Pursuit of Improvement

Empower Yourself – Enhance Your Life

A COMPREHENSIVE GUIDE TO PERSONAL DEVELOPMENT

Derek Dean

Copyright © 2021 by Derek Dean

All rights reserved. No part of this book may be used or reproduced by any means, graphic, electronic, or mechanical, including photocopying, recording, taping, or by any information storage retrieval system, without the written permission of the publisher except in the case of brief quotations embodied in critical articles and reviews.

This book is dedicated to my brother, you are always working on yourself and learning from your mistakes. I hope this book will benefit others in the same way.

CONTENTS

The Journey to Personal Development 1

Unleash the Power of Self-Improvement 3

Using Affirmations to Accomplish
    Your Goals 9

Strengthening Your Weaknesses 27

Developing Laser-Like Focus 33

Setting A Foundation of Discipline 38

Behavioral Growth for Introverts 50

Building Self-Confidence 63

Behavioral Growth for Extroverts 78

Earning Respect 82

The Truth About Education 86

Professionalism 95

Finding an Enjoyable Side Hustle 100

You Are the Money Tree You've
    Been Searching For 112

Viewing the Use of Money as A Tool 116

Optimize Your Living Space 130

Your Community Is an Extension of
    Your Home 136
Multitasking Is A Skill 139
Dealing with Depression and Anxiety 143
Optimism Vs. Pessimism 149
The Right Way to Judge Others 158
Understanding & Accepting Religion in
    Society 162
Handling Addictions and Bad Habits 165
Having Successful Relationships 169
Learning to Think for Yourself 172
Transition from Your Past Self into An
    Improved Version of Yourself 175

The Journey to Personal Development

―――― ∽♋∽ ――――

This book was written to assist people in understanding how they can make simple small changes in their lives and by implementing those things, grow significantly toward being happier and more enlightened about how they interact with the world. If you've been searching to improve yourself by forwarding your personal development, the concepts within will get you there. As long as you're open-minded to new experiences and new routines, this book will open your eyes and your senses to the ways of becoming a more improved and complete person.

Age is just a number. Each one of us matures at a different rate, and some people never do. You are not one of those people, and throughout these pages, you will be accelerating your maturity in many areas of personal growth. As you put the concepts into practice, you'll be honing the skills to make the positive changes necessary to empower yourself and enhance your life.

Unleash the Power of Self-Improvement

In some cases, we arrive at a point in our life when we are prepared to change and improve. Things are not going so well; painful or disappointing events seem to be happening in our lives. I know you understand what I mean: things like continuously picking the wrong partner or the wrong job, or the feeling of being stuck with nothing exciting on the horizon. You start thinking, "I need something else in my life," and you start looking for everything that has to do with self-improvement. It seems like the only time we think about improving is when everything in our life is apparently breaking down, falling to pieces, or we're feeling unmotivated and unhappy—when our minds are filled with thoughts like, "What can I do to change my life and make things better?"

Pursuit of Improvement

There are a ton of things you can do to start improving in your life, and you're doing one of them right now by reading this book. I'm one who believes that once you start making changes, really positive things will begin to happen in your life. You simply have to take action to make useful changes in your life. Self-improvement starts with you, and if you sit back and wait for something extraordinary to happen without making any changes, you'll wait a very long time and never see any results.

The key to personal development is knowing yourself and understanding how you got here and where you want to go. There will inevitably be changes in your life, whether you like it or not. In due course, we will all experience several milestones in our lives. We can choose to sit back watching the world go by, or we can unleash our full potential and power to improve, not because someone told us it's mandatory, but because we don't want a life of feeling unfulfilled, dissatisfied, and without achievement. If you currently feel this way, it's a sign you should include personal development in your life. If you continue to get the same results in your relationships, your job, your finances, your addictions, and other areas of your life, it is a sign that it's time to change and improve.

All the time, I hear people complaining that they hate their life, their job, their partners, or their weight, and yet they decide to do nothing. I don't have time for the whiners who insist that the world owes them because their mommy and teachers told them they are special, and they think they deserve everything because they were spoiled growing up. These people expect life to somehow bend to their will, but they don't do anything to win at life. Even after repeatedly receiving negative results in their relationships and from their half-hearted efforts, they cannot accept that change begins with them. They have to do a self-assessment in their lives and implement improvements, starting with hard work they feel is below them. Everyone starts at the bottom and works their way up, and if you are unlucky and lose the progress in your job you've made over the years, it's possible that you will have to start all over at another business or a completely different sector altogether. Has this happened to you? If so, I think you now know what you need to do.

Watch the signals in your life, and when you see the same warning signs over and over again, take note and start improving. Do not wait for perfect timing before adopting a healthier lifestyle, do it now. You are much more likely to be successful when you see the first signs of a problem and troubleshoot it right away. If your favorite jeans seem to be getting tighter and tighter, start improving your diet. A comparable rule applies to everything in your life. Do not wait until you feel pain and despair before using your power to improve yourself. Don't wait for your world to start falling apart. Many of us do this because change is not always easy, but ignoring it only makes the situation worse.

Unleash the Power of Self-Improvement

Understand that if you keep doing the same things the same way, you will get the same results. Face it and do something about it. Being proactive in your life can be exciting and liberating. It can empower you. Creating positive change through self-improvement will lead to much more happiness, control, and satisfaction in your life.

Perfecting something doesn't mean you have to change everything in your life. Look at the areas that don't make you happy. For example, if you need to shed a couple of pounds, join a rec center to exercise a few nights a week, or you can even check out a free exercise program on YouTube and ask a friend to work with you on it. Make it fun, and you will start to want to improve on it. If you lack confidence or feel that your communication skills are weak, there are so many resources available to help you in these areas. There are hundreds of books, courses, and self-improvement videos that can help you gain confidence and understand how to communicate more effectively.

The beauty of self-improvement is that it is something you can do in the privacy of your own home with many books, courses, and videos to choose from. Develop your path and method for performing solid self-assessments along the way.

When you start to see the encouraging results coming to you because you've decided to unleash the power of pursuing improvement, you will soon realize that this is just the beginning of a much happier and more fulfilled path through life.

Using Affirmations to Accomplish Your Goals

―――― ⸙ ――――

You've probably heard of affirmations before. These are your inner feelings expressed in statements you read or say aloud about yourself. It's like casting a spell and magically, over time, aligning your subconscious mind to these truths in a technique called *affirmative impression*.

Consistently repeating these affirmations day after day will make a permanent mark on your subconscious mind. Once this happens, your subconscious will realize the difference between how you feel and what you see as real in the outside physical world. This difference will provide your subconscious mind with changes to your motivation and behavior to help your outside world begin to match your inside one. It will be magical how the mind's third eye opens and each statement is realized in real life.

For affirmative impression to take effect, affirmation statements must be created in a certain way and completed in a specific order.

First of all, they must be personal and use the first person. Singular first-person pronouns include *I*, *me*, *my*, *mine*, and *myself*. Do not use a second- or third-person pronoun, as in *you* or your name.

Second, affirmations must be positive, with a clear definition. For example: "I eat healthy meals every day." The negative, and therefore ineffective, version would be: "I won't eat junk food every day."

Third, you have to understand that even if the subconscious is a powerful tool, it is still quite simple. Try to look at what you announce as pictures instead of words. When you say, "I will eat healthy meals every day," your subconscious displays a picture of you and the healthy food, and you start to reinforce the healthy or positive behavior.

Using Affirmations to Accomplish Your Goals

Fourth, the statement must be in the present. One might think it makes sense to use future tense, but this is not the case. When you make your declaration in the future, nothing is created in the subconscious mind, and therefore no impression or change will occur.

When you say you'll succeed one day, you're also indicating that you are not reaching your potential now. This is exactly what your subconscious knows to be accurate and therefore, does not change.

By merely modifying this same statement to: "I am successful in my business," you are creating what your subconscious needs to function. These guidelines are crucial for imprinting statements.

So how exactly do you imprint a statement? Follow these instructions:

1. Choose what you want to change. Because you are just starting, select a single subject. Trying to change too many things

at once will significantly reduce the likelihood of something happening. Once you begin to see how the effects of your statement become your reality, only then should you start making a new statement.

2. Write or type your affirmation out on a card so you can see it each day when you read it. Make sure to read it out loud. It instructs your subconscious mind best as a complete sentence.

3. Put the cards in your environment so you see them constantly. Put one next to the bed, one on your fridge, one on your bathroom mirror, one next to your computer screen, etc., in places where you will see them often.

4. As soon as you wake up in the morning and just before bedtime in the evening, say the affirmations out loud. When repeating these statements, speak with enthusiasm and a smile, knowing that

each time you read them, you deepen the imprint in your subconscious memory.

5. Whenever you see one of the cards, read it out loud and believe it to be true, knowing that you will soon see the changes you envision for yourself. When you do this on a regular basis, you will start to see magical changes in your life. So go ahead, do it now. The only thing that can stop you is you.

How to Use Affirmations to Brighten Your Day

Affirmations are the best way to start each day. Everyone wants each day to be a positive and productive day, and one of the best ways to do this is through the use of affirmations. The problem is, people who think about everything they need to do don't always get everything accomplished. It is not enough to only say the affirmations; you also have to live them. You have to start the day positively, end the day the same way, do more than say a statement, do something to make it happen, and be thankful every step of the way. This will create a long series of auspicious days.

Start the Day Positively

The first key to using affirmations to create a positive day is to start the day off with them. Remember only to use present-tense, positive statements. This is the first key to making affirmations effective. When you start the day thankful that your life is good in the present, it is much more likely that your day will be like this all your life.

End the Day Positively

The next key to a positive day is to end well. Supplementing your current and positive views daily will end the day properly. Sleeping in a positive state of mind leads to positive dreams and a more favorable outlook after waking up. Again, this should be done daily at the end of the day in a positive and timely manner.

Don't Just Say It, Feel It

The next key to affirmative work is not only the pronunciation of words, but also the experience of what you say physically and emotionally. This is one of the secrets to obtaining sufficient validation. While you are essentially just saying the affirmation, it is also important to experience what you say viscerally. This is what creates the charm of affirmation.

Take Daily Steps

The true secret to having continuous positive days through affirmations is to act on them. I suggest you do something every day to guide you in the direction you want to go. You actively have to work on what you want to be. Knowing that you are living your affirmations and taking action every day will lead to more positive days.

Be Grateful

Affirmations relate to what you will have in an affirmative and present way, but it is only out of gratitude for each day that all things are positive. Find a small reason to be grateful. If you have a significant victory in a project, be grateful. The key is to be thankful for all the positive things that happen, big or small. This will help reinforce the positive days you experience.

Start the Day Off Right

Today is the building block for tomorrow and the start of the rest of your life. From there, you can choose to be happy and engage in a life of luxury and new experiences, or perhaps prefer to continue where you left off the day before. Either way, every day offers endless opportunities and the opportunity to take your life to a whole new level.

Starting a day with a solid routine can be the difference between a good day and a miserable day. Most people wake up and participate in tasks assigned to them by outside forces. Wouldn't it be nice to wake up and feel you are in control of the day?

Well, these ten morning practices will help you start your day off right and get work done at an optimal level.

Smile

Starting your day with a smile is a great way to celebrate the fact that you are alive. The very fact that you wake up and live another day is a gift in itself. So take the time to enjoy the sun sliding through your blinds or the comfortable bed where you've had the chance to sleep all night. Studies have shown that a smile releases endorphins, natural pain relievers, and serotonin. Together, they make your body feel good.

Breathe/Meditate/Pray

Deep breathing, prayer, and meditation can bring many benefits to the human body. Controlled breathing helps relieve tension in the body by lowering blood pressure. It also oxygenates the cells of your body, improving the quality of your blood and eliminating toxins.

Humbling yourself by being thankful you have the blessing of life will give you the courage to face the day ahead. When you meditate you have to tune your frequency to the things you want to have in your life and repel any negative frequencies invading your thoughts. Meditation can help clear and calm your mind, preparing you to problem solve and think critically about what needs to be accomplished.

Make Your Bed

Making a bed is the first necessary but direct task of the day. Show that you are proud and disciplined. Getting out of bed and preparing it for later is a small win to start the day. You will feel accomplished as you start the day, which will put you in a more focused mood to get other things done as well. It will also look better when you enter your bedroom when you return home following a busy day.

Self-Affirmation/Visualizations

Affirmations are short sentences or positive compliments you say about yourself. They help you focus on your best qualities. An example could be: "I have fun wherever I go because I like to interact with people." Daily repetition will help you reprogram your brain and make you believe it to be true.

Visualizations help the body prepare for what the mind has already accomplished. The brain cannot distinguish between something that happened and something that was imagined. In other words, just visualizing your day will not only change your mindset but also prepare you to move through it. This technique is useful for professional athletes in their sports or businesspeople on their way to work.

Stretch/Exercise

Starting the day with a pleasant morning including some stretches or exercise will make you feel good. It improves circulation and increases flexibility. It doesn't take more than a few minutes, but the effects will last all day. It will surely wake you up and improve your coordination. This is precisely what you need to add that little boost to your stride when you walk around the office.

Morning exercise will amplify the effects of the stretch. It's challenging to get into a routine of getting out of bed to run or do push-ups and abs. However, if you can finish a fast run at six in the morning, you can cope with all that the day has to offer.

Drink Water

The human body is known to be mainly made up of water. So why deprive your body of something so desperately needed? Drinking a glass or two in the morning is exactly what the body needs. Remember that hydration is extremely important for feeling good throughout the day!

Have Breakfast

The eight hours you spend sleeping are technically one-third of your day. Although you may think you are not hungry when you wake up in the morning, your brain needs glucose to function correctly. So even a small energy bar can make a big difference in brain functioning. Unless you are intermittent fasting, breakfast is an important way to start your day.

Read an Inspirational Quote

Take a minute to read your favorite inspirational quote. It's a great way to get a new perspective on something or set a goal for your day.

Listen to Your Favorite Jam

Music activates the brain in several places. They include the auditory cortex of the brain and the limbic system. This can help you recover specific memories or simply prepare for the day ahead. For thousands of years, music has been part of human culture. Who doesn't like to start the day with their favorite song?

Set Goals

Each day, you must complete a specific task or goal. Aimlessly, people get lost and react to the world in which they live. Action must be the engine of your life. Without a clearly defined route or destination, it will be much more challenging to know what to focus on to achieve your goals.

Start your day with some, if not all, of these morning practices. To do so, you will need better time management and discipline. But the results they produce will far exceed the extra time required to achieve them.

Frequently Asked Questions

Few people use positive affirmations daily to achieve their goals. However, positive affirmations are used by some of the most elite and influential people in the world to achieve goals in many areas of their lives. There seems to be confusion as to why to use affirmations and whether they work. In this article, I will answer a portion of the most frequently asked questions about their application.

Aren't affirmations just words on paper?

Affirmations are not just words on paper. These are powerful words by which you can create a positive belief in your mind so you can have any of the desires and successes you see for yourself. Statements that are made daily including actions in line with them can help you achieve any goal.

How do affirmations work?

The way affirmations work is to give your mind a belief system so you can achieve your goal. Talking about affirmations daily helps build a positive mindset, which is essential to achieving any goal. There is a saying: "You have to believe in getting there, way before you get anywhere." If your mind is not ready and you cannot see how you are achieving something, then you cannot make it happen. But if you can change your state of mind into positive affirmations, you will start to believe you can accomplish a given task and then achieve it.

How many different declarations should I make?

I would make them in all areas of your life you wish to change. There are several areas where you can create affirmations for, for example, spiritual, emotional, business, family and health and fitness. After determining which areas you want to change, grab a piece of paper and pen and think for 10 to 15 minutes. Search your thoughts and brainstorm what you want to change in your life and when you have all the positive statements you can think of on a particular subject pick the one you feel you want to tackle first . Once you have identified the most positive views in each area of your life, write them down until you have a complete list of areas you would like to see changed. Then decide which is the most important to do and write your affirmation.

How many times a day do I have to reaffirm?

It is best if you can spend at least two minutes focusing on your statements every day in a calm environment. Whenever you feel depressed or negative, this would be another good time to say your statements. You will understand that once you have expressed your point of view, you'll be very positive and feel that you can conquer the world.

What time of day do I have to reaffirm?

I would say positive affirmations for at least two minutes a day, one when you wake up and another before bed. If you think this is not enough, continue with your statement and say it every time you start to feel negative. If you spend two minutes each day focusing on the statement, your comments will help you start the day off positively and get work done during the day. This should help you maintain a positive frame of mind to achieve your goals. Another good time to express your statements is just before you go to bed. This will help you maintain a positive state of mind before bed and will help you sleep better at night. You can also say your positive affirmations throughout the day if you feel cynical or unable to complete your tasks.

Now that we have answered some of the most frequently asked questions about affirmations, it is time to start constructing your essential statements so you can grow and prosper. It is a simple but powerful technique that has been used by many powerful people to succeed. So if you're someone who feels negative and like you can never reach your goals, give yourself a chance at positive and productive affirmations. I know your life will change for the better.

Strengthening Your Weaknesses

———— ～♋～ ————

Identifying your weaknesses shows your strength of character and determination. You can only improve if you accept that your skill set is less than ideal. Take into account your strengths and weaknesses and then move forward with a strategic improvement plan. Personal responsibility may seem daunting, but the risk is worth the reward. If you can act and turn your weaknesses into strengths, you will become a much stronger person and a role model for others.

Benefits of Understanding Your Limitations

Start by making a list of your weaknesses. Make a list of everything you think needs improvement. If you have trouble identifying specific weaknesses, consider things that put you at risk or cause you to be disappointed with your performance. Next, organize your identified weaknesses into categories, which can make them less prevalent. For example, if you want to be bolder, more honest, and more visible, create a statement that will work with your "affirmative skills." Finally, identify the areas where your weakness stands out, so you can develop an improvement plan.

Define Aims

Set goals to create an action plan to improve weaknesses. Make sure your objectives are explicit, quantifiable, feasible, practical, and timely. Improvement is difficult to measure, but do your best to take note of your steady advancement. Break it down into manageable goals. Assign a deadline for each purpose. Be realistic in your objectives to ensure they are achievable. Your list of goals acts as a strategic plan to improve your weaknesses. This will also help you prioritize what is most important to work on first.

Get Additional Training

Professional development is a crucial action you can take to improve weaknesses. When you review your goals, identify areas for improvement that require new knowledge and practice. Many organizations offer free training or even finance external courses. Use your written action plan to justify why your employer should support additional training to help you reach your full potential at work. Mention specific training programs that allow you to fill a knowledge or skill gap. Some training courses include proactive ways you can improve to strengthen your professional portfolio.

Strategic Advice to Improve Your Career Plan

The best way to enhance your career is strategically. Look at what you can do to have a meaningful impact on your career. Are there simple strategies you can apply that can have an immediate positive impact on your career? If yes, what are they?

One such strategy you might find helpful is a self-reflection strategy. It sounds simple because you can do it yourself, as long as you are open-minded and true to yourself. While these systems are straightforward, they must be practiced in the event that you are willing to make a change.

However, there is a word of caution. There is nothing that can improve your career if you feel that there is nothing you can improve. Being stubborn and closed-minded will hinder your ability to grow.

<u>Define Your Approach</u>

I have always championed defining your approach as proud, passionate, and having belief in yourself. Do everything you do with pride, passion, and confidence, supported by skills, knowledge, and direction, and followed by action—and you will go far

Further, diligence, humility, and honesty are essential to advancing your career. Working hard is relatively simple. It just means that nothing comes easily. There is no reward in the world that comes without hard work. There is nothing in life that truly matters, which comes without putting the time in. You'll be surprised at the things you can accomplish when you continuously take baby steps in the right direction toward reaching your goals.

Modesty comes with maturity. When you know you don't know enough, you start being a student again. If you want to improve your skills and knowledge, then go for it! It will enhance your life and your career.

Are you doing your job honestly? How do you manage your colleagues? Is it with integrity? Do you recognize your mistakes and not blame others? Honesty is not just about others. It's also about being honest with yourself. Can you manage your mind? Are you afraid of facing your helpless weaknesses? Are you afraid of facing your lack of strength? Being honest with yourself leads to awareness. The initial step to propelling your profession is to define your attitude.

Awareness

Monitoring your qualities and shortcomings gives you a fundamental advantage over most other people, and on the chance you need to improve something in your life or your career, you can. This awareness is self-reflective. Think of something that makes you feel inadequate. This feeling of inadequacy creates an innate need for improvement.

The energy created from this awareness is the positive energy that drives you with the confidence to improve yourself. Recognize what needs to be improved and understand what you need to change. This is a simple strategy that can help you enhance your life.

Developing Laser-Like Focus

―――― ⁓⦂⁓ ――――

Every day you make choices about what is most important to you. Focusing is the way you decide where to expend your efforts. Do you want to focus on your work projects, your relationship, your chores, or a hobby? One big problem in today's world is you can start to focus on things that are less important than the things you should be focusing on. Why would you give extra effort and energy to something less important? Because it's simply more fun or enjoyable. This is where you need to think; use your mind and focus on the most important things in life first. Then you can have all the fun and do whatever you want.

I'm going to tell you about an idea I came up with called the Levels of Focus. The levels are based on the things you need to accomplish in everyday life and are ranked by how much they demand your immediate focus. For example, if

Pursuit of Improvement

you wake up on a weekday with an hour before you need to leave for work, even though you really want to finish a quest in a game you've been playing, the Levels of Focus come into play, and you realize that there are more important things to get done before leaving. You need to make your bed, shower, wash up, get dressed, and make your morning coffee or other breakfast. Since those things take priority and are required your focus, they are on a higher level than your video game. In another scenario you might be really hungry, but you have an item you need to mail out, and the post office closes in twenty minutes. Using the Levels of Focus, you will forego making something to eat and make sure you are on time to the post office before they close. Then you can go back home and make something to eat.

Focusing on the Most Important Things First

In today's world we are constantly bombarded with distractions and notifications that are vying for our attention. If you want to succeed in life, then you need to harness the ability to focus on one task until that task is finished. This is called *laser focus*; it's the mindset that allows you to tune out the rest of the distractions in your life and really lock into a super-productive mode that lets you start and complete tasks faster than other people because you are not consistently bouncing your focus from one task to another and back again. This problem, which most people have, is called *shiny object syndrome*. It means they are drawn to whatever thing in their life seems to be the newest and most interesting. This can be as simple as a notification on a phone letting you know a friend has messaged you or a recent news article that popped up alerting you of something that just happened. It could also be that the project you've been working on for the last three months hasn't made you any money yet, and you hear of something that might, so you drop all the work you've done so far to start a new venture. Only after you are successful in a task should you be moving on to tackle other tasks you have set for yourself. If that means long nights working on a side job before any real income comes from it, then so be it. Writing this book was a situation just like that for me. I had to stop everything else I had planned in my life for a few months and spend my free time coming up with ideas of what to write about. Then I decided which of those ideas would end up making it into the book. I would then sit for hours to write each chapter and make sure what was being said would be beneficial for anyone reading it. Even after finishing the book and publishing it, I knew my intense focus must not be deterred. If no one knows my book is available to purchase and learn from, then I've just wasted my time writing it. Most likely you came across this book because after finishing it, I put my time and money into marketing and advertising it. This is how you must approach any task in your life. Decide what outcome you want for yourself and focus intensely on that task until you are able to make it a reality. An acronym for remembering how to focus and get the most out of your life is FOCUS (Follow One Course Until Successful).

Setting A Foundation of Discipline

In all situations life throws your way, being able to have full control of your thoughts and actions is an invaluable resource. Understanding and controlling your mindset and emotions is essential to your overall well-being. When you get angry or upset or show negative emotions, you cannot make the right choices or decisions. Your emotions activate chemical reactions in the brain that can affect your thinking. Once your brain starts to function abnormally, it cannot see the situation at hand as it should, because it is in an altered state.

Do you remember when you had a contention with a friend, family member, or coworker and knew that the conversation was going south to the point of one of you starting to yell at the other? While this is one of the many universal experiences that all people share, there are things you can do to avoid it.

Setting A Foundation of Discipline

The most effective way to avoid a power struggle or a fight that you don't need to be in is to change your approach. You have to have discipline, so you don't get carried away by your emotions. Discipline helps you get what you want out of life. You have to understand that being able to alter your situations is extremely powerful and, when you do, it will also bring benefit to your interactions with others.

If you are able to take a moment and realize this conversation is going to end up in a fight, discipline will assist you in keeping composure and either coming up with a solution to avoid the verbal argument from escalating or just walking away so the two of you can cool off a bit. Whatever topic it was, can best be revisited at a later time.

Remember, the conscious mind accounts for 10 percent of what we believe, and the vast 90 percent comes from the subconscious. That means you can say to yourself in your mind, "I wonder what process Jenny is going to take tonight." Then if it starts again, you will be ready to control the conversation and calm her down so you can discuss the matter in a calmer way. By doing this, you can produce an outcome you both agree on better than when you both were hot-headed. Only once the discipline to do this is established can you think clearly and assess the situation, eventually coming to a more favorable outcome.

Adjust Your Mindset to a Successful Way of Thinking

If you care about career development, hard work should be a priority every day. However, hard work may seem unjustified if one's expectations are not fulfilled, and this is where self-discipline comes into play. Self-discipline allows you to control your actions and emotions and finish the work at hand regardless of how you may feel about it. The thing is, you always have control over your performance and responsibility for the quality of your work. It also includes a commitment to oneself and career, one that is independent of the circumstances or uninfluenced by the situations that arise, no matter how challenging it may seem at the moment. This will allow you to be disciplined and know that your best performance depends on continuous effort, which establishes the mentality of your personal and professional success.

How Discipline in Itself Is a Form of Success

Being disciplined can have many descriptions, including working hard, maximizing productivity, or staying focused on what needs to be achieved. The most significant correlation between a concentrated mindset and effort is the development of superior performance. This definition of work speaks in-depth about doing the best you can. It strives to maximize your return with your current skills and abilities while being open to learning and investing just the right amount of effort.

There will be times when you are most certainly not at the top of your game, and that is certainly understandable. There will be days when you will work the best you can, and there will be days when you will do your best. The importance of discipline means that you do not allow working conditions to determine your productivity. If there are new policies you need to adapt to, additional business requirements, or other circumstances, you can always control your actions and aim for maximum performance in the context of professional development.

Learn to develop discipline as a way of thinking about how you work every day, and see how your career continues to grow as this sense of self is reflected in the results you experience, personally and professionally. The most effective way to control your career and establish a model of success is to control the way you think and work. Self-discipline is a productive mental state and a concentrated attitude that you can implement now. When you work to the best of your ability every day, you will be intellectually impervious to unfavorable conditions and prepared for new vocation opportunities. When you are intellectually disciplined, you and your career will be transformed.

How Discipline Affects Your Career

Developing a disciplined mind sets you up for success, while a lack of deliberate discipline prepares you for failure. Self-discipline is based on a logical and rational perspective, focuses on control, and encourages the use of productive work habits. It commits you to professional development and makes it easier to have concentrated effort in accomplishing tasks.

Without self-control, an individual is bound to be hasty and unfocused, to react emotionally, and to be reactive to circumstances. It's easy to start working on self-discipline, whether it's a habit or not, if you begin to create the proper intention then you will make it your goal to reach your highest level at all times. Self-discipline does not require prolonged effort, only a constant sense of purpose and the occasional understanding within yourself that certain things are more important than others. You can make decisions based on what is best for your current environment, at any given time. Self-discipline involves maintaining control over your attitude, mentality, emotions, and thinking at all times.

Your work has a specific description or at least an expectation of what you should achieve. With daily tasks, you can use discipline to determine what effort is required to complete the tasks required of you, and that will be enough to make you feel good when the workday is over. However, some circumstances influence the amount of effort you have to put in. You may have too much work, an upcoming deadline, or a person with authority who is pushing you to take extra steps. In these cases, you can either willingly or reluctantly do more than you want, but your career is at stake.

The attitude you develop toward your business will affect the development and progression of your career. If your job performance involves minimal effort, it will be accompanied by feelings of job dissatisfaction, which can create a negative mentality about your career. This means you see your energy from the perspective of what you get from work now, not what you can get from it in the long run. When you are disciplined, you maintain behavior and an attitude that enhance your daily productivity, which also gives you the confidence to stand out even when circumstances are not perfect.

Learn to Develop Good Intentions

How do you feel good about your job and maintain that attitude, even when the circumstances do not please you? You can't compel yourself to feel constructive feelings when some occasions or individuals provoke negativity or frustration. What you *can* do is change your perspective, and this is where self-discipline is paramount. You can decide that you will feel good as a professional or as an employee despite the current conditions and create a position statement focused on your professional goals. This will help you create a disciplined mindset with purpose and focus.

Your career is a series of steps and progress that will occur over time, and for some, it will be achieved through multiple jobs or careers. The essence of this is you as a person, and you are the one who can learn and grow. With deliberate intention, you can view each job as a springboard that provides skills, knowledge, and direction. If a post does not meet your expectations or becomes problematic, figure out what you have obtained from it, give this information in your resume, and decide your next step. But whatever happens, always make sure you have a disciplined approach toward your work and career plans.

Consider How the Employer Sees Your Disposition

Think for a moment that you are a hiring manager. What kind of candidate would you consider for a job if you looked beyond the job description? Would you consider someone whose tone showed evident frustration and who didn't seem to have much to say positive about their current employer or their current job? This is not a likely candidate for most employers, based solely on their attitude.

Now think of a candidate who enters and is professionally present, shows a clear understanding of his career or objectives, and can articulate what he has learned from each job he has done throughout his career. This is a candidate that is likely to increase your interest as a hiring manager, because they have demonstrated a disciplined mindset.

The purpose of reviewing these scenarios is to show the contrast between someone who has a fundamental sense of importance or career control, which also shows the difference between a disciplined and undisciplined mentality. If you want to be a candidate who gets a job, set the goal of being highly disciplined and productive.

Your mood will be transferred to the tone you transmit when talking to potential employers, along with your general professional attitude. Someone who is disciplined and sees all messages as a learning experience has confidence in their identity and the gifts they have, paying little mind to working conditions or circumstances.

How to Develop Your Approach

You can begin to develop a diligent and self-disciplined mindset by first exploring career plans. If you can't articulate the details of your career, now is the time to start. At least, opt for a short-term and long-term professional objective. This will give you direction, one that can help you find what you can learn, instead of focusing on existing working conditions.

Setting A Foundation of Discipline

The purpose of developing a career plan is to give it the ability to create a specific purpose. When you enter work every day, you can remember that you can learn from any situation, even if what you learn is you don't want to continue growing or advancing in your current career and instead want to change it.

Learning and growth: an essential component of discipline is to maximize your learning and growth potential. If you have developed a productive working relationship with your supervisor or manager, ask them if there is more you can do. For example, you can start a new project based on the needs of the department or the company. For some, this may seem counterproductive and an attempt to become a "master pet," but it could also be the determining factor to you being seen as a valuable employee and getting a raise or promotion over your other peers.

Behavioral Growth for Introverts

In a world where extroverts grab everyone's attention, being an introvert in society can be a little more challenging. Break out of introversion and learn to welcome the balance of extroversion.

Introversion has many benefits in the workplace, such as the ability to focus on one task until it's finished, change the world, and achieve higher levels of profitability. Quiet, contemplative people are usually the best software engineers, the best screenwriters, and the best producers of artwork.

At the same time, the challenges are many. Introverts can be extremely antisocial, which means that they often cannot connect with other people and have difficulty expressing themselves while communicating. They tend to prefer being alone or with a friend or two over being in a large group of people.

Remember, while you can't change your DNA and it's perfectly fine to be who you are, there are simple ways you can make small adjustments to get more involved in projects, communicate more effectively, and develop stronger leadership skills.

What Makes You an Introvert

If you like minding your own business instead of meeting friends or attending social events that you don't care about, you already know that you're introverted. If the outward expression of your feelings is uncomfortable for you, know that being an introvert is not that bad. While you may not be able to cope well in certain situations, you may find yourself exceptional when dealing with others.

This personality trait called introversion is characterized by a miserable social life, but by many internal feelings which are generally not expressed. Not only do they introverts tend to exaggerate and fear each interaction beforehand, but they can also feel helpless when surrounded by other people. Here are some additional signs to check if introversion is a personality trait of yours:

Signs of Introversion

You enjoy your own business and feel safe, relaxed, and comfortable in your own space to do the things you enjoy. Your mind is more noticeable when you are alone. Social interaction can expose you to the high stress you are trying to avoid. The only circumstances in which you can focus on the things you love are when no one bothers you.

Interacting with individuals isn't your thing. You want to get things done independently from anyone else, tune in to your music as opposed to speaking out. Headphones are always your companion. Music distracts you from anyone who wants to torment you. As long as you don't have to listen to others, you feel better and enjoy every moment.

On the chance you have ever encountered any of these feelings, you know introversion can cause numerous difficulties in daily life, and you would probably like to overcome these unpleasant situations. Regardless of whether you appreciate your time alone, there are times when you want to enjoy the company of others without feeling stressed or uncomfortable.

Best Practices to Escape Your Shell

As was mentioned earlier, being an introvert is not a bad thing. Even if some situations can overwhelm you, you should know that there are others you can handle incredibly well. Your personality is not only inviting but also intriguing. Others may not understand you all the time, but there are some facts about you that may surprise you.

You often do not have small talk conversations because you prefer more in-depth discussions. As an introvert, you usually avoid talking to others, but when the right subject

Pursuit of Improvement

arises, you are ready to share your thoughts and experiences in a way that surprises everyone.

As an introvert, you may sometimes think you miss the benefits of extroverts, but in fact, introverts have a wide range of skills, like everyone else. The misconceptions that circulate don't have to scare you. If you want a smooth transition from introvert to extrovert, there are a few essential tips to remember that can support you, extending your limits of comfort.

This process should help you communicate better with others, get rid of the shyness that causes discomfort and stress whenever you are around other people, and help you avoid feeling drained when at parties or work. Seek out the best advice for introverts to make your life easier.

There are many ways to interact with people, and little by little, you can start to answer the question, "How do I stop being introverted?" You need small steps to get used to the social interactions that scare you. The following tips will teach you to balance extroversion and to have the confidence to spend more time around other people.

Steps You Can Take to Become More Extroverted

Just Say "Hi!"

Perhaps the ideal approach to defeat modesty is to try to start short conversations with people you know, just by giving them a "Hello!" It is the surest way to show people that you are present, that you have noticed their presence, and that you are ready to speak to them. With each interaction started with "Hi!" or "Hello!" you'll be surprised at the people you can meet just by saying something so simple. Plus, you can play a little game and challenge yourself to greet random people on the street and see what's going on. You will be amazed to see that numerous people will hear your greeting and strike up a conversation with you. The more you do it, the less uncomfortable it will be.

In conversation, follow "Hi!" with "How are you?" They will likely reply with good or great. Then they might ask you how you are, and you can do the same. If the conversation doesn't go on from there, you should be the one to extend it by asking, "How was your day?" or "What did you do today?" Then you can share your experiences with them and find common ground to speak about just about anything from there, whether it's sports, a similar hobby, or current events.

Make Eye Contact

The process of becoming an extrovert also involves changes in attitude. Even if we are talking about small gestures that go unnoticed, you will be surprised to see others react to them. One way to overcome shyness is to look at others and make eye contact. Try looking into the eyes of the person you are talking to for a few seconds. There is a tip you can use if you don't feel completely comfortable at first. Try looking at their other facial features, like eyebrows or hair for a few seconds, then back to their eyes. Just repeat this anytime you feel direct eye contact is too much for you.

Exercise with People You Already Feel Comfortable With

Even introverts have people with whom they always like to talk and with whom they can open up. Attempt to begin a discussion with someone you are exercising with, whether at the gym or while playing your favorite sport. Getting to know people you interact with every day can help you build friendships in the future.

Find the Social Situations That Suit You

The right social environment will have a significant impact on how you start conversations with people you don't know. If you are not an entertainment fan and you are invited to that type of event, it will not be easy for you to find common interests with the people there. However, if you are an animal lover, a trip to a local kennel could bring you interesting topics to discuss with the people you meet there. Try to find the right activities and socialize with people who understand your interests and you can feel comfortable with. This could be the key to overcoming your shyness.

<u>Join a Class or Club</u>

Talking about the things you love will make you open up more to others. It can be a book you like, a movie you've watched, a sport you're good at, or your profession. People who share similar interests will give you enough confidence to raise your voice and find joy in spending time with them and others. Join a football team in your area, join a yoga class, or attend a weekly meeting of a local book club and give yourself plenty of opportunities to talk about the things you are interested in. You will be surprised to know that you want to talk more and more. It's good practice, it's comfortable, and it's one of the best ways to overcome shyness.

Mentally Change How You Approach Certain Situations

If you want to work on becoming a better communicator, use this useful tool to force yourself to speak with others. Whether you're at home or the workplace try to make a phone call for every five emails or text messages you send out to people.

Introverts are usually hidden at the back of the room. They slip in unnoticed, take a back seat, and then don't speak in the crowd. Do not do that. Come early to the meeting and try to meet your colleagues or raise your hand and comment on the subject. It is surprising how a little effort can open up interesting opportunities. Go ahead and try it. No one is judging you as much as you think they are. They are much more worried about themselves.

Attending events where you don't know anyone can be stressful. The key is to get into an event and find someone there who looks friendly or interesting to talk to. Go up and say: "Hi!"

Introduce yourself and tell them why you are there. They will then reply with their name and do the same. Now that you've instantly made an acquaintance, try that two or three more times. Then when it's time for the event to start, you can sit or stand next to one of the people you have just met. If you want, you can write their names on a notepad or add them to your contact list on your smartphone, so you don't forget them. This forces you to be sociable, giving you a goal everywhere you go.

None of these steps is difficult. They are wholly achievable and practical and easy to work into your day. You can also add any other changes you feel will help you open up. If you work on this over the next few weeks and feel that you are progressing, keep at it until you feel like you've achieved the comfort level necessary to turn on a little extroversion anytime you need to.

As you can see, introverts can be happier in many ways, not only with themselves but with others. Finding a balance between introversion and extroversion can improve your mood, and therefore your life, in a way you never dreamed of. Having more friends or people you can talk with and share your feelings and thoughts with will make your life much better and help you reach a higher level of happiness.

You've discovered how to overcome shyness, you've seen the importance of talking to others, and now all you have to do is put this life-changing advice into practice. With a little courage and a willingness to add social interaction to your life, the process from introvert to extrovert can be easy and a pleasant escape from your comfort zone. What's more, before you start thinking about whether it's worth it or not, try to remember that what you're feeling right now isn't what you always want to feel. It's good to enjoy being alone and having quiet time to yourself, but also understand, life has more than that to offer. Coming out of your shell every now and then can greatly benefit your life and help you obtain characteristics of extroversion as well.

Building Self-Confidence

―――― ❦ ――――

Accepting yourself is the key to feeling comfortable in your own skin. Confidence allows you to see yourself as you are and not allow other people's views of you to dictate how effective you are at doing things you want to do. Confidence is the overall mental ability to walk into a room with your head held high and speak to others around you without hesitation.

From time to time, we all feel shame, a flash of discomfort that makes us want to hide and never face the world again. But when these thoughts repeat themselves, or when we are afraid of being made fun of, or we avoid certain situations because we are worried about how other people will judge us, that shame can lead to paralyzing anxiety.

We can first overcome feelings of shame by understanding what causes them, and then by learning to accept ourselves as we are.

Pursuit of Improvement

Acceptance is not easy, but it is essential for living a happy and fulfilled life where we are no longer ashamed of who we are.

Shame leads to anxiety when we continuously think about our past and feel ashamed that we have done something or said something "wrong." You often feel guilty because you believe that you are not equal to others and that they do not integrate with you.

You can also set high expectations for your behavior, demanding you achieve perfection in everything you do.

An alternative to trying to be perfect and "integrate" is to accept ourselves as we are. Self-acceptance can help us because when we genuinely believe that we are fundamentally sound and fair individuals in spite of our faults and flaws, we can free ourselves from the fear of doing or saying something we are ashamed of.

By accepting ourselves, we discover that even if we have different feelings, wants, and needs from others, we are worthy, fortunate, and complete as we are. March to the beat of your own drum. Make decisions based on what you want, not what you think will make other people happy.

Why Isn't Accepting Yourself Straightforward in Modern Society?

We learn to accept ourselves in a culture in which hard work, effort, goal setting, and self-improvement are highly valued. We are encouraged to be ashamed of our wrinkles, our excess weight, our lack of purchasing power, our clothes, our belongings, and almost everything we can think of.

Our culture plays with this fear that we will not be good enough, to sell us "remedies" for our pain. These drugs come in the form of antiwrinkle products, diet pills, brand-name clothes, and gym memberships or self-improvement classes.

Pursuit of Improvement

There is nothing amiss with attempting to adopt new things, improving your skills, and improving your emotional and physical well-being, but it has to come from a place of accepting ourselves as we are.

A child does not learn to walk ashamed to crawl; the child learns from curiosity, determination, and the desire for development. There is no problem with purchasing the things we want, as long as a feeling of inadequacy doesn't motivate our consumer spending.

Buying a nice shirt or elegant dress for the pleasure of wearing and enjoying it is entirely different from buying a product because, at a deep level, you feel insufficient without them. If Nike shoes are more comfortable than other brands, buy them for that reason and not because the Swoosh or Jordan logo is thought by others to be cool.

How to Achieve Self-Acceptance

Sadly, there is no speedy method to get this feeling of self-acceptance for many. It is a process that can be slow and frustrating. But the simple fact of knowing that you have a choice, that you don't have to be ashamed, and that it is not your duty to feel guilty for each offence, slip, or hiccup helps to alleviate the burden of guilt a little.

To help you progress toward self-acceptance, when you feel embarrassed, try to relax and breathe. Then do your best to resist the temptation to follow the negative emotions and realize that you are who you are and you cannot change most of the things you are worrying about. When you come to that realization and understand your faults, focus on your breathing again and relax knowing everything will be okay.

Continue to relax through your sense of shame, whether it's from your hair not being brushed, acne scars on your face, being too short or overweight. These are issues many people have to deal with on an everyday basis. Do this inner assessment of yourself until it becomes second nature to react in a positive way. Over time, you will begin to accept yourself for who you are. Some of the things that bother you can be fixed over time and others can't, but in the moment, just live your life and don't give a care about what others might think about your appearance or inadequacies.

What Happens When We Begin to Acknowledge Ourselves as We Are?

Imagine the relief, the weight off your shoulders, when you honestly believe that you are adequate regardless of the constrained assets in your bank account, the car you drive, the clothes you wear, or how you look.

This beautiful way of life is a blessing to us, and it is ours to enjoy as we will. We can choose not to pay our precious time, energy, and attention to becoming what society deems acceptable. We can decide to dismiss the message from large businesses that play on our fears of not being sufficient to sell us their items. Think of the late Steve Jobs from Apple. Even having a high net worth, all he ever wore every day was a plain black shirt and jeans. We can all learn a little something about confidence and simplistic minimalism from him.

We can decide to accept that our qualities, thoughts, ideas, and feelings are as valid as those of any other person and release the belief that there is something in us that is not acceptable. We must do all of this while being aware that we have the right to do whatever we want and not care if we are judged by others for doing so.

Small Actions to Build Confidence and Overcome Shyness

Stand up straight, with the best posture possible, shoulders back, stomach in, and chest out. Holding yourself this way helps you exude confidence. Standing in a corner with your head down and arms folded may not be the best position to invite people to speak with you. Remember to stand up straight and look people in the eye. Not only will you look attractive and safe, but you will also feel that way.

Set goals and reach them. Using the tips above, you don't have to change everything in one day. It will be a gradual change from a self-observer to a smooth, outgoing person. Small steps will help you improve your social skills and dare you to be in the spotlight.

Smile. A smile can change everything. Not only will you look more friendly, but people will also feel better about you, and it will make others smile too. You can start a chain reaction that will brighten up the day for everyone around you.

Kill negative thoughts. This is perhaps the main reason why you tend to doubt yourself when you try to communicate with others. All the fears start in your mind and make you stay silent, afraid of being ashamed. Try to ignore any negative thoughts that overwhelm you, and you will feel more secure and happy. Try to take these negative thoughts as a challenge, remember your past, and try to imagine the great treasure that awaits you after overcoming these challenges.

Speak slowly. Social interactions can scare you and make you overthink when you speak. When you talk slowly, you give yourself time to think about what you are saying, rather than letting quick, negative thoughts flow through your mind. Also, speaking slowly is a hallmark of those in authority who believe in what they say and leave others with the impression that it is worth listening to.

You may have never thought that a few small changes could have such a positive impact on your confidence and the way others perceive you. As E. E. Cummings said, "Once we believe in ourselves, we can risk curiosity, wonder, spontaneous enjoyment or any experience that the human mind reveals."

Feeling good about yourself will help you find the courage to leave your comfort zone, dare to speak more often, and get more involved. In psychology, there is an unofficial concept that says people start to see themselves in a better light and have more confidence if they act like they have it from the start. You can build trust and happiness in your mind by working as if you already have these things, and as a result, people will start looking at you as such. Who doesn't want a happy and secure person in their life?

Powerful Ways to Increase Self-Confidence

Confidence gives you the strength to conquer the world. This is how you can learn to trust in everything you do. Confident people admire and inspire confidence in others. They face their fears and are willing to take risks. They know whatever obstacles they face, they can overcome them. Confident people tend to see their life in a positive light, even when things are not going so well, and they are generally satisfied and respected.

Wouldn't it be astonishing to have this sort of confidence every day of your life? Guess what? You can.

Low confidence is not a life sentence. Self-confidence can be learned, practiced, and mastered, like other abilities. When you ace it, everything in your life will improve.

— Barrie Davenport

It all comes down to the direct question: if you don't believe in yourself, how do you expect someone else to do it?

Try some of the following tips. Don't just read them and put them in the back of your mind. Start practicing them daily, starting today. At first, you may have to pretend to have confidence in yourself, but over time you will begin to feel that confidence growing inside you. With a little time and practice (this is not an overnight phenomenon), you can also be comfortable with yourself, inside and out, and exude a confidence others will admire.

Get Away from Negativity and into Positivity

Now is the time to assess those around you, including your friends and family. It's difficult, but it's time to seriously consider distancing yourself from those who failed you and destroyed your confidence. Even a temporary break from Debbie Downer can make a significant change and help you take steps toward a greater you.

Be positive, even if you still don't feel it. Invest positive enthusiasm in your interactions with others and start running, excited to begin your next endeavor. Stop focusing on the issues for a mind-blowing duration and focus on the solutions to make positive changes.

Change Body Language and Image

Little by little, you can adjust your posture, show a smile, give direct eye contact, and talk more confidently to other people. The simple act of putting your shoulders back makes you feel like you are a more confident person. A smile will not only make you feel better, but others will feel more comfortable with you. Imagine a person with the right attitude and a smile, and you will envision someone who is confident.

Look at the person you're talking to, not their shoes: maintaining eye contact shows confidence. Finally, speak slowly. Research has shown that those who take the time to speak slowly feel more confident and appear more confident to others. The advantage is that others can understand exactly what you are saying.

Go the extra mile and trim your hair, give yourself a clean shave, and dress well. Not only will you feel more comfortable with yourself, but also others will see you as successful and secure. Tip: when buying a new suit, have it professionally tailored to fit you perfectly. A tailored suit makes all the difference in the world when trying to make a good impression.

Pursuit of Improvement

Try not to acknowledge disappointment, and dispose of any negative voices in your mind. Never surrender, and never accept anything less than your best. There is a solution for everything, so never throw in the towel. Make it your new mantra. Succeeding through big problems will create a significant boost in your self-confidence.

Low self-esteem is often caused by the negative thoughts that continually cross our minds. If you are constantly upset and say that you are not good enough, that you are not attractive enough, that you are not intelligent or athletic enough, and so on, you are creating a self-fulfilling prophecy. You become what you preach in your head, which is not good. The next time you hear this negativity in your head, immediately change it to a positive affirmation and continue until you reach the goal of increased confidence.

Be Prepared

Learn everything there is to know about your field, your business, your presentation, and everything that follows on your "to-win" list. If you are willing and able to support it, it will increase your confidence.

For Stressful Times When Everything Else Fails, Make a Good List

Life is overflowing with challenges, and there are times when it isn't easy to maintain confidence. In those times, sit down and make a list of all the things in your life you are thankful for and another list of all the things you are proud of. After you've finished your records, put them with your affirmations on your fridge's door, on the wall next to your desk, on your bathroom mirror, somewhere where you will quickly remember the beautiful life you have and the fantastic person you are. If you feel that your confidence is diminishing, look at these lists and take them to heart, and you will be inspired again.

Behavioral Growth for Extroverts

———— ⁓✒⁓ ————

What traits make you an extrovert? If you are sociable, outgoing, an action taker, and an attention seeker, then you exhibit the traits of an extrovert. Extroverts love meeting new people and feed off the energy of others, prioritizing social gatherings versus being alone. You'll usually look to others for your source of ideas and inspiration throughout the day and enjoy sharing your thoughts and feelings with whomever is around. Friends will be easy to come by, but you will also rub some people the wrong way, even if it's not your intention to do so. Your outgoing nature combined with attention-seeking qualities can be both a blessing and a curse. Depending on who you're talking to, being overly funny or sarcastic can leave a stranger wondering if you were being offensive to them or not. Use your senses and try to understand the people around you and how they might perceive your words or actions toward them.

How Extroverts Can Work to Refine Their Behavior

Extroverts experience the exact opposite feelings as introverts. They feel more energized around other people and prefer social situations to being alone. These are amazing traits that most introverts wish would come naturally to them. But just like introverts can work on becoming more extroverted, extroverts can also learn from introverts about how to balance out their behavior and improve how others view them in the world.

Extroverts can learn a lot from their introverted counterparts, starting with the ability to process a thought before saying it out loud, which is probably the most important of all for them. Remember that it's better to refrain from commenting unless what you have to say is positive and encouraging or a complement to the others around you. "If you can't say something nice, don't say anything at all."

Being alone can be bothersome to people who exhibit extroversion at their core. These people can especially benefit from the topics later discussed in this book about peaceful meditation techniques and the qualities of a Zen mind.

Learn to be one with your thoughts and allow them to flow through you instead of being so eager to share them with everyone around you.

As an extrovert, challenge yourself to listen twice as much as you speak. Regardless of what you believe in, whether it's creation or evolution, your body has been formed with two ears and one mouth.

Give yourself time alone each morning to plan out your day and what you would like to accomplish. Then at night take some time alone to reflect on the day you just experienced: the people you met, the things you learned, and all the unexpected things that happened. These quiet times will help you prepare for days ahead and also to process what's happening in your life.

All of these things will help you to become a more complete person, helping you to balance your inherent extroverted nature.

Earning Respect

―――― ˞ˢˤ˞ ――――

Respect is treating other people the way you want to be treated. It's as simple as that. All you have to do as you go through your day is think about each individual interaction with others as if you were interacting with yourself. Be pleasant, courteous, and helpful, if need be, to the other people around you. In turn, most of those people will see your actions and return the same courtesy.

In tribal times, we lived with nature surrounded by trees, plants, and animals in a very close community where everyone was familiar with everyone else. Presently, we are still encompassed by parts of nature. However, the individuals primarily represent the living energy that surrounds us in everyday life. One imperfection I noticed in this social scenario has to do with the way humans look at and treat each other now.

Earning Respect

Surrounded daily by people in suits and work clothes who rush to work or mothers with their children at the store, there are so many faces that if you tried to take the time to connect with each of them, you would go crazy. What I'm saying is that the people you are continuously interacting with on a daily, weekly, or monthly basis should be treated with respect. You don't need to treat them as friends or acquaintances, but treat them as people, just as you would like them to treat you. If you see someone in need, help them. If someone needs advice, give it. Be open to the people around you and do what you can to make society a better place to live.

How often do you realize you deserve as much respect and attention as any other member of society? Why have we lost this demonstration of acknowledgment from other human beings? You would probably answer that, "We are too busy to think of a stranger who seems to have little connection with our goals in everyday life." But if we were to truly understand the importance of each moment and each person with whom we interact in our lives, we would begin to see life as something unique and magical. Even in everyday situations, every moment we have is an opportunity to learn more about and positively impact the people in the world around us.

It is time for us to realize once again that each person we come into contact with is another person, an individual in their own way with feelings and emotions just like we have. What I would like to see is more attention given to your fellow man, which means doing everything possible to treat everyone with sincerity and respect.

How to Gain Respect from Others

It is not easy to gain respect from others. Respect is something that is built over time but can be lost in an instant. Once respect is lost, it's one of the hardest things to regain. When you lose someone's respect, that person has a new view of who you are. They won't be able to return to their previous view of you until you work really hard to repent for whatever you did to lose their respect in the first place.

We all want respect. Respect is earned through a combination of several factors: willpower, patience, perseverance, and integrity. Find out what steps you can take to gain respect from those around you. Pay attention to the details, the people you know, their names, and the things they say. Remind them of the details of what they said in a previous interaction or use their name when addressing them to leave a lasting impression. They will feel valued, and they will start to treat you the same way in return and respect you too.

The Truth About Education

When we think about the word *education*, we immediately think about kindergarten through twelfth grade and college. But what is education really? Education is anything we learn throughout our lives. You can be educated about how to drive a car, fix broken electronics, or do search engine optimization. No one can ever learn everything, so learn about the things that interest you or will benefit you, and forget about the rest.

Growing up, we become educated in numerous things we don't even think we're learning about. This is because we are watching what other people are doing and emulating what they do. This is essentially an education. As we grow older and graduate from high school or college, we've all learned the same set of things, from reading and writing to history, science, and arithmetic. Whether you got A's or F's in school is arguably irrelevant. The knowledge you took away from those years is completely pointless when it comes to everyday adult life.

Only a few of the things you mastered will benefit you the rest of your life. Hopefully you can read and write and have basic math skills. Excluding some extremely specialized careers, you will never need to know how to do calculus and algebra or the significance of numerous historical dates and scientific theorems. The most useful thing we learn, if anything, from all the years at school is how to learn. Very few things taught in school can prepare you for the real world and the responsibilities you will have once you start needing to take care of yourself. The really crazy thing is, not before we graduate but only after we graduate does the real education necessary to succeed in life begin.

I would argue that for most people, going to college after high school is a huge waste of time and money. The thousands of dollars is not worth the cost of instead having those four years to do something worthwhile, like learning a trade and getting on-the-job training or starting your own business. The only way a college education is worthwhile is if you are planning to go to post-graduate school for a specialty, like becoming a doctor, lawyer, or engineer. If you are not going to college with a set purpose and an expectation of seriously sticking to your vision of becoming a specialized professional, then you are essentially going to waste four years of your life. A business degree, like so many people default to, is not worth the time or energy. Do you know how many people are coming out of college with a business degree these days? The student loan debt you will put yourself in will take a really long time to pay back unless you are one of the few lucky ones to land a great-paying job. There are a ton of degree choices, but very few are actually worth even getting to begin with.

If after reading this you still decide to go to college, research everything you plan on accomplishing there. Make sure the degree choice you choose is a direct stepping stone to your future success, and like I iterated before, it most likely isn't going to be unless part of that future includes higher education after college in a post-graduate school program. You need to seriously weigh all your options and decide if you will be getting the best ROI (return on investment) or ROT (return on time) over the four years you spend there.

What Is Education Really?

Education is the sum of your knowledge and experiences and the ability to use them to succeed in life. Once you graduate from college, it is your responsibility to educate yourself in the areas you see as important to you. Does that mean learning how to do handyman work or doing your own oil change? Maybe it means you want to learn about the stock market or investing in real estate. When you truly understand education, you realize that it never stops unless you want it to. Do you want to be versed in the world around you, or do you want to stay ignorant to these things? That is solely your choice to make, but the more you know and understand about the world, the better your chances of having a successful life.

Places You Can Go to Educate Yourself

Let's start out with the most basic place you can go to educate yourself. your city or county library. Your local library has an abundance of books on just about every topic you can think of. How did anyone learn anything before the invention of the internet? They went to their library and took out some books on the topic. You can ask a family member or friend who may be knowledgeable about a certain topic to train or teach you. One of my favorite ways to get an education is through an in-person course or online webinar. The internet as a whole is a great source for gaining knowledge about things, whether you ask a search engine like Google or Bing, join a Facebook group, or watch an instructional video on YouTube. However, you need to be wary of your sources. Just because you read something on a blog post or see it in a YouTube video doesn't mean it's just as simple to accomplish. Sometimes you need to understand that the people writing these blogs or putting videos up on YouTube are benefiting from your clicks, likes, and watch time. So they will say things without telling you the whole story about how they got to that point. It's extremely easy to sell something if you have a hundred thousand subscribers, but if you are starting out with none, then good luck. When you learn about something from one source online, try to cross-reference it with other sources online as well. Then you can determine if what they are telling you is the whole truth or only part of the truth.

The Education Conundrum

Don't let me scare you, but here is the biggest issue learning things yourself can create: it becomes an almost endless rabbit hole of things to learn. Let's say you want to start a business. Now you need to learn how to get an LLC created, set up a website, and design business cards and a logo. What about how to sell and advertise? It is possible to delegate these tasks to other people, who you can find on websites like Upwork or Fiverr. Then come additional costs with each new thing you learn about that needs to be done or created. This is the same for other things, too, for example, art. You can draw, use paints, clay, or metals, but each of these things requires more and more education, and each has its own subset of knowledge. What kind of paint should I use, watercolor or oil pastels? What about golfing? Do I use a driver or a wedge? Depending on the slope of the green, should I try to place the ball in front or behind the hole? So your education will continue long after you leave school, and learning new things will always be a part of your life.

How to Learn

Learning, believe it or not, is a skill like any other. We need to practice the things we learn, or we might forget them. It isn't enough to put half-hearted practice into something. You must have perfect practice, meaning you are doing it to the best of your ability at all times and not just going through the motions. This goes for learning any new skill, whether it's how to use a software program or how to shoot a basketball correctly. You can learn how to use Adobe Photoshop in a lackluster, half-caring kind of way and only understand a few of the features, or you can truly learn it and master every aspect of it. Same goes for shooting a basketball or swinging a golf club. If your form isn't perfect every time you practice, then when you need to execute in the game, you'll be less likely to do so. Ever heard about day-trading stocks? You will fail miserably if you do not have perfect practice with the concepts over and over again, understanding each and every movement, and even then, you're not guaranteed to be successful. A little bit of advice: don't try to day trade stocks unless you are willing to lose all the money you started with and possibly more. Only 10 percent of traders are successful at day-trading. If you do try to tackle this feat, start out with a free-money paper trader first to hone your skills.

I know you are the type of person who will take this advice to heart, because you picked up this book, and hopefully you will never stop learning and trying to improve yourself. Whether it's emotionally, financially, or physically we all have room to improve in our lives and a lifetime to learn all we challenge ourselves to understand about the world. A healthy life is full of challenges, and an education into the topics you are working to master is the best way to find the solution for them.

Professionalism

You must be a professional in the workplace. It is one of the most important criteria used by superiors to assess your overall performance. Peers will also judge you by the professional standards you show in the workplace. Professional ethics are critical in any business environment. They also play an essential role in the advancement of your career. You will get a job over another person if a potential employer thinks you present yourself in a more professional way.

Professionalism is not just about wearing proper corporate clothing. You can show you're professional if you do the following:

Maintain mental stability. Keep your cool regardless of whatever stressful situations arise over the course of the day. It is essential to communicate well with everyone in the office. Be direct but courteous. Avoid too much emotion when communicating with colleagues or managers.

Be smart! A talented employee knows what to do and how to do it. Remember that hard work is not enough. Being intelligent means meeting and exceeding the expectations of your superiors. Respect works both ways. Respect the organization, its managers, and associates, and hope to receive the same level of respect in return.

It isn't nice to make annoying comments or jokes that hurt someone's feelings. Never refer to personal appearances, ethnic groups, gender, or religious practices when around your coworkers, or any other time for that matter.

Always be honest. Dishonesty will not only result in termination, but it also can ruin your future job prospects. After being fired for cheating or stealing, you will have to find another job, and without a great referral from your previous employer, this will be all the more difficult.

Professionalism

How to Dress Appropriately

A good appearance will make you feel good inside can help you project the right image. Since you are looking for a professional and elegant look, it is essential to wear clothes that reflect the current trend, favor your figure, and reflect your personality. When buying a new work wardrobe, make sure it contains elements that mix and match, and purchase pieces in neutral colors to make the overall look more presentable. Always try to buy the best-quality materials possible. They will last you much longer. If you look and feel flawless, it will be easy for people to see you as safe, reliable, and credible!

Let's start by making an excellent first impression. When you first meet someone, it takes little time for them to form an opinion about you, not only based on what you wear, but also based on your body language, behavior, manners, voice, and even posture.

Pursuit of Improvement

Try to be open and confident: use your body language to project reasonable confidence. Get up, smile, make eye contact, and say hello with a firm handshake. All of this will help you project confidence, and if you are calm and confident, the other person will also feel more comfortable.

If you don't think you can do that, it is good idea to practice positive visualizations: see how confident and secure you feel in meetings, see how others react positively, and remember how you feel. Imagine taking control, and people respecting you and your opinions. Think about the empowerment that this implies. Try to create not only the scene you need to see but also to attach emotions, to feel how strong and safe it is, to explore how you can do what you decide. In addition to allowing you to overcome your fears, doing this will also attract positive situations for you. The law of attraction positively attracts, and you get what you truly believe in.

Be positive in your attitude toward work and life. Even when people criticize you, try not to

Professionalism

defend yourself. Take it with a positive attitude and take what you can from it. Try to stay poised and keep a warm, authentic smile!

Lastly, I want to mention something about having good posture, probably one of the simplest yet most important ways to look professional. It's one of the very first things people notice about a person, whether it's a conscious thing or not.

Finding an Enjoyable Side Hustle

More and more people are working a full-time job while working a side hustle simultaneously. A side hustle is a flexible business that makes money, but more importantly, it can be a job you enjoy working. A lot of people think about starting a side hustle but never actually do it. Nothing happens in life unless you take action, so quit thinking about it and start one today.

First, it will generate additional income in addition to your main job you have to pay all your necessary bills with. Second, it allows you to explore a passion that you cannot explore much in your main profession. Are you a musician? Maybe teaching music after work can be a relaxing way to make extra money. Are you am an artist interested in interior design? You can be an independent interior decorator. Fiverr.com and Upwork.com are great websites you can use to start a side hustle from home and over time possibly even create a full-time income from things you enjoy doing every day.

The third reason some people take up a side hustle is to test if they can move into another professional field. It's a great way to explore another professional opportunity without giving up your primary job and find out if it's something that will work for you.

Read below to find out how to find the right placement for you. Likewise, see a point-by-point rundown of ten extraordinary thoughts for potential ideas.

Tips for Finding a Side Hustle

Assess your abilities. If you want to make extra money but don't know what to do, think about your skills. Is there something you are particularly skilled in that you cannot use at work? You can be an influential writer or editor. Try to search for independent writing or editing work. Maybe you've always been good with animals. You may consider walking dogs or taking care of pets. Think about the skills you have and use them.

Think about your passions. In addition to thinking about your skills, think about what you are passionate about. Do you do a lot of fitness and wellness? Consider getting certified in yoga classes and classes at your local gym. Are you passionate about education? Become a teacher in a subject you know. Make sure your side hustle is something that interests you genuinely so you can enjoy the extra work.

Manage your time. Before pushing ahead, make sure to balance your time. You need to make sure you can still succeed in your first job. Think about how long a second job will take you and when you can do it. Is there something you can do in the mornings before work or in the evenings after? How about on the weekend? Make a schedule that will allow you to balance both jobs effectively.

Finding an Enjoyable Side Hustle

Top 10 Ideas on the Side

Below is a list of ten side job ideas. These would be good ideas for different reasons. Some are exceptionally adaptable and enable you to make a calendar that works with your primary business. I know there are many others as well, but hopefully this list will give you an idea about what I've been talking about and get you moving in the right direction to pick one that fascinates you.

E-Commerce

You can sell stuff online, and there are many sites that can help you accomplish this quickly and easily. If you're an artist of sorts, consider selling your products on Etsy. If you want to purchase used products at low prices, you can turn around and make a profit reselling them. You can also refurbish products, such as past years' technology, and sell them on several sites, the most popular being eBay.com. If you're going to be completely independent, you can create your own website and sell products there. This kind of work gives you incredible adaptability because you can make and sell products by yourself.

Provide Care

Some people feel that they like taking care of others. If so, consider providing daycare or prekindergarten services in your area. There are also many options for caring for the elderly or disabled who need help during the day. Finally, if you're better with animals than with humans, you could help take care of someone's pet. You can offer services for walking or grooming dogs. You can provide these services directly to people you know or take advantage of many websites and applications that support them. For example, Care.com will allow you to offer babysitting services to others, and Rover.com will enable you to find people looking for dog sitters and walkers.

Event Planning

Are you known among your friends as an excellent party organizer? Are you organized and give great attention to detail? Consider offering your services as an event planner. You can help plan anything from children's birthday parties to business events or weddings. If you are not interested in event planning, consider playing another role in the evenings, depending on your skills. Consider starting a small restaurant service or (if you have a musical inclination) offer your services as a DJ. If you're a good baker, offer pastries (like cakes or cakes) for parties and events.

Photography

Do you have a passion for photography? Maybe you like taking pictures with your family or friends? Think of photography as your lively side. You can bid on taking family portraits or photograph events like weddings.

Real Estate

Are you interested in real estate and home improvement? For starters, if you own a home already, you can start by repairing and remodeling yours. You can also buy houses with the intention of fixing them up and selling them. On the chance you want to become a property investor, you can buy and rent homes or apartments. You can also obtain a real estate license and become a part-time real estate agent. This type of work is relatively flexible. Finally, if you are interested in renting part of your own home for a short stay, consider signing up for Airbnb or another website that lets you rent a property.

The Service Industry

The service industry is a significant sector, but many people find it challenging to help others. Companies like TaskRabbit allow you to research and provide services ranging from fulfilling orders to repairing a broken sink. You can also offer delivery services. Companies like

Instacart or DoorDash can help you with this. Finally, if you have a car, you can provide your driver services via Lyft or Uber.

Teaching

Teaching is a broad category that addresses many different options. If you are a specialist in a particular academic field, you can teach students in the subject or give an online lecture. If you play an instrument, consider teaching music. Are you passionate about fitness? Consider teaching yoga or other fitness classes. The advantage of these side hustles is that they are truly adaptable. They likewise enable you to impart your enthusiasm to other people.

Travel Guide

If you live in a city or other area frequented by tourists, consider offering your services as a travel guide. All you need is a little information on the history of the place, a friendly and open personality, and strong oral communication skills. You can offer your services with family or friends or join sites like TourByLocals.

Web Design

Do you have programming and web-design skills? Many companies are willing to pay people to design or modify websites for them. It is also flexible work that you can do in the evenings or on weekends when you are not working. You can also do this type of work from your home.

Writing and Editing

Are you a good writer? Use your writing skills. You can edit academic essays for students or write and edit website content. Many companies self-publish their works online, and you can edit those. If there is a point that interests you, consider creating a blog based on the subject.

Side Jobs Can Lead to a Career Change

A side job can be a springboard for a career change in many ways. Not only can you connect with new clients and potential partners, but it also offers opportunities to learn and improve the skills you need to advance your career.

There aren't many good jobs that require no previous experience. Any business you apply to will ask what your qualifications are for the position. If you are thinking about starting a new career, you must start today to develop the skills necessary to get that future job.

In the case you don't have the chance to advance these skills in your current job, you may find a side hustle that allows you to learn them. Finding a part-time, flexible job is the best way to find a new career that interests you. You can find out if you really want to continue spending your free time developing these skills, or you can even learn to look for something different.

Whether you want to improve your skills to progress full time or start running your own business, the skills you develop in your side work will also be a great learning experience and useful for your future.

Pursuit of Improvement

And if you want to be your own boss, starting slowly with a side hustle is the perfect way to prepare for success. You can learn all the great lessons of running a business while maintaining the safety net of your main business. A sense of security and a "must-succeed" attitude gives many entrepreneurs the courage and persistence to grow their side hustle to bring in the income needed to cover their entire monthly expenses.

First you learn, and then you earn. You need to have an endless hunger to succeed, and everyone has the same twenty-four hours in a day. You can either spend your free time and weekends binge-watching TV or playing video games, which will only keep delaying you from reaching your real goals, or you can lock in to being productive and do whatever it takes to achieve your dreams. I'm not saying you can't have any fun or relaxation along the way. I'm saying there needs to be an understanding in the back of your mind that your goals won't achieve themselves, and you're the only one who can decide how much time you want to delegate toward accomplishing them.

You Are the Money Tree You've Been Searching For

What is a money tree? A money tree is a business that makes you money, all day long, even while you sleep. *You* are that tree! You have the ability to become the business you seek. Become an influencer by creating quality content on any topic you want to talk about. Post it on YouTube, Instagram, Twitter, Facebook, and any other social media platform you can think of. There are other people who share the same interests as you, and those people will watch your content. Most importantly, create video content, but other content will help you expand your reach online as well. Start a website blog telling people about your topic. Then when you have enough subscribers, you can take time to make a digital course teaching about it. Write a book you can sell to your followers or make money advertising to them. Companies will pay you to promote their products and give you a percentage of the sales you are able to drive to them. You can create your own products on Teespring.com, including apparel, home decor, and mugs too. You can do all of this starting with your smartphone or computer camera. As your subscribers grow and you start seeing some profits come in for your videos, you can reinvest some of that money into your business to buy more professional lighting, backdrops, and cameras.

You can talk about any topic you are knowledgeable about, but if you want to make the most money, choose a topic based on relationships, health, or wealth. Channels based on finance make the most money overall, but the other two choices are also terrific topics to create your channel on.

If none of those options seem to fit your expertise, don't worry about it. You can create a channel based on sports, news, comedy, cooking, doing makeup, playing video games, and even reaction videos to your favorite band's new releases, etc. If you have an interest and a specialty YouTube is a place where you can share that expertise with the world.

Keep at it! Don't quit! New channels have to put in a lot of work before they start seeing traffic and subscribers. You need to keep posting as much content online as you can and as often as you can. Eventually people who share the same interests as you will come to watch your content, and as soon as they do, you will start to see your money tree grow. The more people who watch your videos, the more the YouTube and other site algorithms will favor your content. Then the sites will suggest your content to viewers even more and rank it higher in search results.

By building a personal brand or channel and gaining a large subscriber base of people who look up to you and value your opinions about whatever topic you are speaking on, you'll be able to monetize that following over and over again through all the options I gave you and more. No one finds a money tree already grown and flourishing, but if you are willing to start with nothing and believe in yourself, then you can plant the seed within yourself to slowly grow over time. For some people, it may be a few months, and for others, it may be a few years. The average YouTube channel doesn't start to gain any real traction for upward of six to nine months, so you need to be diligent and continue posting content until you see that people are starting to subscribe to your channel. The financial reward you will reap in the long run from having a successful YouTube channel will outweigh the painstaking time it took to build a strong following from nothing. Once people see you as a reliable expert in your field of expertise, you'll be creating a business with the opportunity for multiple streams of income, and from that point on, your money tree will grow continuously every day and night.

Viewing the Use of Money as A Tool

Money only has value because as a society, we give it an assigned amount so we can use it as a medium in the exchange of goods and services. Whether it's paper or representative digits on a screen, money should be used as a tool to gain things we couldn't have or don't have the time to create on our own. Think of every dollar as a worker, and when you spend it, you are using that worker to get what you need. You can only spend a dollar once, so be aware of what you are accomplishing when you choose to spend it.

Are you in the mood for a nicely prepared meal? Go to a restaurant. Do you need a new pair of pants in the correct size? Go to a clothing store. Want to invest in a business? Buy a stock. Almost anything in life you could take the time to create for yourself is purchasable using money as your

Viewing the Use of Money as A Tool

tool. Is it possible to cook up a great dinner from scratch? Sure it is. Can you buy a sewing machine and make your own clothes? Of course you can. Can you gain the knowledge to start your own business? If you're willing to put in the time, the answer is yes.

There is only so much time in a day, and each person has their talents to monetize, so you don't have to be proficient in everything. Some of us are great cooks, and some of us aren't. Learn to accept what you do best to make money, and then use that money as a means to an end to get what you need. This is why everyone needs to have a job or a business, so the money can continue flowing and be used for your everyday wants, needs, and bills.

Monthly bills in most cases can be reduced to give you extra money to spend on stuff you need. You can choose a different internet service, phone provider, landscaper, or insect prevention company by calling around and seeing what competitors are charging for similar services.

Check out different car insurance providers to compare current rates before your six-month renewals come due; they are constantly changing. Depending on current rates, you can even look to refinance your mortgage. By doing all these things and more, depending on what you're paying for each month, you'll be able to maximize the amount of money left to purchase other things you'd like to have.

How should you be spending your leftover hard-earned dollars? Each of us can only make so much money over the course of each month. After you've paid for your recurring monthly bills, you should set money aside for daily needs such as food to eat, necessities such as toilet paper, toothpaste, laundry detergent, and finally, clothes to wear. The money you have left over after all that's been allotted is considered discretionary. This means you have the ability to spend it wherever you want. When using this discretionary money, always ask yourself if what you are buying will be used often. If you are buying something that will end up sitting in a drawer or collecting dust on a shelf, let someone else buy that item, and use your funds to purchase something that will get used over and over again. This will make the money spent well worth it. I'd even argue that if you know you are going to use an item over and over again and get continued use out of it for a very long time, then you can even willingly overspend on an item like that, rather than one which will get used less or won't be as enjoyable to use in the long run. An example of this would be to save up money for a good-sounding set of Bluetooth earbuds versus an inexpensive pair, which you'll get some use out of but will ultimately want to replace soon after you buy them.

If you want to have a higher net worth in the future than you do now, one thing you can do with the leftover money from each month is to invest it.

Put Your Money to Work for You

Don't let your money sit in a savings account. Every year your money will be worth less than it was the year before due to inflation. Inflation generally reduces the value of your money by 2-3 percent each year. Set aside money you don't need to use for the month and start slowly building an investment portfolio. By investing in stocks, you will grow your money over time. Warren Buffet, one of the top stock market investors of all time, said that stocks transfer wealth from the impatient to the patient. You must be patient with your investments. Markets fluctuate up and down, but you can only lose money if you sell a stock when it's down. Do not sell stocks when they are down. The market will bounce back in the future; it always does. When you look to buy a stock, research the company first and only purchase it if you feel you'll want to own that company for the next ten to twenty years.

Viewing the Use of Money as A Tool

No one has an excuse not to invest in the stock market anymore. There are simple-to-use apps you can download on your smartphone to buy and sell stocks for free with no transaction fees. These apps include Webull, Robinhood, and M1 Finance. I actually use all three. Webull is the most intermediate of the apps. Both Robinhood and M1 Finance allow for the purchase of fractional stocks, meaning you can own and invest in any stock you want for as little as a dollar. Don't have the money to buy Google or Amazon stock? Don't worry. Just buy as much of the stock as you can as a fractional share and take part in the stock market on your own terms. M1 Finance even allows you to set up an investment pie of all the stocks you want in your portfolio and will auto buy the stocks in the percentage you preset for them, every time you make a deposit. Over time the fractional shares will become full shares of these amazing companies you didn't have the money to invest in all at once, but over time you'll have a nice portfolio of company stocks you own. Don't buy lottery tickets; buy fractional shares instead, and if you pick dividend-paying stocks to invest in, then you'll get paid a small percentage of the total value, usually paid out quarterly by these companies. You can then reinvest the dividends into even more stocks, and your portfolio will grow on its own over time between the money you put in, stock price increases, and dividend reinvestment.

If you are able to start investing in your twenties and thirties and want some additional advice outside of purchasing individual or fractional stocks, you can set aside up to $6,000 a year in a Roth IRA, which can grow to over a million dollars by the time you retire in your fifties and sixties and will produce a nice nest egg to live off of the rest of your life.

You can consider buying Bitcoin or other cryptocurrencies, such as Cardano or VeChain, as a store of value with real-world applications as a hedge against the dollar and inflation. Don't shy away from buying small percentages of

Bitcoin. Just because you can't own a full Bitcoin, it should not deter you from slowly over time dollar-cost averaging into it. Even a hundred dollars a week or month will grow over time, and in just a few years I'm sure you'll be surprised to see how much you have gained.

These crypto markets are measured with candle charts the same way stocks are, but that is really where the similarities stop. Cryptocurrencies are another layer of the internet, and each has its own unique parameters and goals. They are coded into the blockchain to guarantee transparency and trust in whatever purpose they're used for. These projects fluctuate at a much more volatile rate than stocks, and that is an important key to understand when buying or selling them.

When you decide to get into crypto, there is a learning curve about how to transfer dollars into digital currency. Depending on how much money you are investing, you might be able to pay with a credit or debit card, but more often than not you will need to link a bank account and wire funds to a bank connected to an exchange such as Binance US or Kraken. Then after you purchase crypto on the exchange, you can move it from there to a dedicated personal wallet. Some wallets are hot, meaning they are held on wallet apps connected to the internet and protected by passphrases and passwords. Never share your passphrases or passwords with anyone unless you want them to have access to your funds. Others are cold, meaning they are taken completely offline and stored on physical wallet devices. When you make the decision to enter the world of crypto, you are taking full control of your assets, so be very careful to protect all of your recovery passphrases and passwords because losing them will mean losing access to your funds. Do your own research and make sure you understand what you are getting into before committing any of your hard-earned money into cryptocurrencies. Eighty percent of day traders fail, so try to pick cryptocurrencies you believe in, and then plan on holding them for the long term, as in three to five years, and watch your money grow. Some crypto offers an incentive to stake for an annual percentage yield, otherwise known as an APY. By taking advantage of this, you can reap rewards from a few percentage points to over 10 percent, depending on which coin or coins you plan to keep your money staked in.

Investing in real estate is another great way to make your money work for you. You can choose to buy properties to rent for consistent cash flow, or you can buy homes to fix up and flip for a profit. These strategies are very different from one another. If you choose to rent the home, rent it out as is or do very basic repairs. Upgrading a rental too much can be pointless given that a nicer place might rent out quicker but will most likely not command a higher monthly rent than one that isn't as nice with a similar amount of space in a similar area. Flipping a home is the exact opposite. You are looking to upgrade the property as much as possible, still allowing for a nice profit, so you can bring it up to par with other homes in the same neighborhood and sell it quickly.

Investments use the money you put in and work for you all day long, even while you're sleeping. Whether it's a stock or a real estate purchase, in most cases these assets will be worth more when you sell them.

Do not start investing if you have any credit card debt. Your extra money is best used to pay off that debt first. If you have a spending problem, I would only use a debit card for a while and forget about using a credit card until you have your spending habits under control. Do not use credit cards for investments. Credit cards should only be used for purchases you already have the money for and should be paid off weekly or monthly. Credit card benefits like cash back or reward points are only worth getting if you are paying your card off by the due date. Never carry a balance on a credit card. The interest rates these card companies charge is usually around 20 percent, which can be twice or three times the rate you would normally be looking to get from one of your investments for the year. A good stock investment portfolio will normally see gains of 7–10 percent per year on average, and home prices in a good market can be expected to grow at a similar rate.

Assets versus Liabilities

Assets are things which make you money. Liabilities are things which cost you money. Assets increase in value over time, and liabilities decrease in value over time. Education is an asset because it will make you more money. If you buy and hold stocks for the long term, they are an asset. A successful business is an asset, and purchasing real estate can also be an asset. If you own the home you live in, then it is a liability because you are paying a mortgage on it every month, but if you are renting the home out or buying one to flip and make a profit on, then it's an asset. A car is only an asset if you are using it to make money; therefore most cars are liabilities. If you use your computer to make money, it's an asset. If you use it to play video games and surf the internet, then it's a liability. I think you get the idea. The more assets you have, the more your net worth will become. Spend your money creating or acquiring assets, not liabilities.

How Money Is Used as a Tool Against You

There is no such thing as a free lunch. If someone tells you they are giving you something for free, then it should raise red flags and set off alarms in your mind to figure out the real reason they are giving you something for nothing. If you are getting something for free or even at a discount, then in the majority of cases there is an ulterior motive by the person or business giving it away. Generally, they are doing so to pull you in and gain your loyalty for the future. It's good to be aware of the hidden reasons we may be offered things for free. Whatever you get for free or at a discount cost something to produce, so time or money was spent in order to gain your

Viewing the Use of Money as A Tool

loyalty. Once you choose to spend your money with a person or a brand, you are more likely to spend money with them again in the future, especially if you feel like you got a bargain from them the first time. Now that you know this, you won't be taken advantage of, and if you want, you can use this knowledge in your own dealings with others.

Optimize Your Living Space

As the saying goes, cleanliness is next to godliness. Take a moment and realize how messy and disorganized your house becomes when there is no daily cleaning. Most of us don't have a maid coming each week to keep our home clean and tidy. Dirty clothes, dishes in the sink, and the accumulation of dust around, etc., can only contribute to stress, hide bacteria, and create odors. The most important rule for organizing a house is to have an organizing and cleaning routine. This is essential for maintaining a safe and clean home environment. The best day of the week to set up this routine is the day before trash day, or if that isn't good, a day you have off from work. I understand no one wants to do extra work on a day off, but it's imperative to keep a clean home to be happy and have a stress-free life.

Optimize Your Living Space

It is essential to keep your house clean by making sure you finish cleaning a room before moving on to the next one. First, take the items that are on shelves and give them a good wipe down before placing them out of the way. Now is an excellent opportunity dust all areas. If necessary, clean the glass, sinks, tables, or other surfaces around the room. Then vacuum and make beds or put things back on the shelves. Only after everything is done should you take out the trash. Repeat this process when cleaning all other rooms in your residence.

Room cleaning procedures prevent you from wondering which room has been cleaned or needs to be cleaned. This can create more relaxing moments for you and save you a ton of energy. You can store cleaning products at all levels of the house, including in each bathroom and kitchen. This can make the cleaning task more convenient and efficient. Therefore, you can always be ready for a cleaning situation that requires your immediate attention. Visible spots that seem to appear all the time don't look good on anything. Teach the people you live with the basics of cleaning a home. Ask them to practice good hygiene and cleanliness. If you are not alone, split up the chores between everyone so they are easier to complete. Collaboration with other people living in the same residence can make it easier to keep your house clean and manageable.

A pro tip for a single person who is very busy and hates the time it takes to clean a whole house is to schedule specific rooms to clean over the course of the week, with each on their own day. This way, it will only take you twenty to thirty minutes to clean the "room of the day," so you don't have to spend a couple hours cleaning and doing the whole house all at the same time.

Why Making Your Bed Is So Important

It seems so easy to leave a messy bed when you wake up in the morning. After all, you're just going to mess it up again the following night.

Optimize Your Living Space

Making a bed has become one of those daily chores that people struggle with doing each day and therefore tend to overlook. Let me remind you that a properly made bed dramatically affects the appearance and feel of a room. For starters, it helps make the room appear less chaotic. It also sets the stage for your night's sleep. Getting into a made bed at night feels so much better than trying to straighten out the indented pillows, intertwined sheets and blankets from the night before.

Making your bed every morning is also an important mental step to beginning the day. It's that very first task you can complete quickly and easily, starting you off on a positive note to get your other more important tasks for the day done as well. Each completed task during the day, big or small, is a successful achievement that creates a sense of accomplishment within you and an energy that flows into whatever else you need to get done. Just imagine the energy you can build heading into your day when you successfully wake up on time, make your bed, shower, wash up, do your hair, get dressed, have breakfast, and are still out of the house on time. Your energy for that whole day is stronger than if you had slept late, skipped making the bed and taking a shower, thrown some water on your face, brushed your hair, grabbed a quick snack, and showed up late for work. In that case, the day would drag on for you and you'd be stressed out until you got home, all because you didn't get started in a way to build up the necessary positive energy for the day.

Take Time to Fold Your Laundry and Put Dishes Away

Folding laundry is another thing some people hate to do, so they take their clothes and stuff them into drawers. Then when it's time to wear them again, they take them out and have to iron them. It's so much easier to fold your clothes to keep them neat and tidy, so when you need to wear them again, you can take them out of the

Optimize Your Living Space

drawer, and they are ready to put on. This also goes for clothes in the closet. If you don't hang them up, they most likely will get wrinkled, and you most likely will not like the way they look the next time you want to wear them.

We use glasses, cups, dishes, bowls, and utensils every day, but when we're finished using them, they end up on the kitchen counter and in the sink. Take time at the end of each meal, or at the very least, at the end of each day, to put them into the dishwasher, so they are out of view and in place to be cleaned overnight.

Taking care of your home, making your bed each day, folding your laundry before you put it in your drawers, and putting the dishes into the dishwasher each day will keep your home neat, tidy, and organized throughout.

Your Community Is an Extension of Your Home

We don't just live in our home. We live in a neighborhood community which is part of a larger area, city, or town. Don't litter when you're out and about. Keep whatever trash you might have on you and wait until you can dispose of it responsibly in a trash or recycling container. Of course, there are people being paid by the government to keep our cities and towns safe and clean, but we all have a personal responsibility to aid in keeping our communities safe and clean places.

If you see someone in distress, like a car accident just happened in front of you, stop to see if they are okay, or at the very least call 911 to report the location of the incident. If you see a hit-and-run and you can remember the license plate of the vehicle, call the authorities to report the crime. Give aid to those around you who might need it, like help an older lady cross the street, return a stray dog to its owner, or hold the door for the person behind you. Always be courteous to the other people around you, including when you're driving through the community. If you see a tree branch or other obstruction blocking the street, instead of just driving around it, cautiously stop and move it to the side out of the way. If you're out for a walk and you see trash by the sidewalk, pick it up and dispose of it. We all need to do our part in keeping our communities clean. Be aware of the things around you and pride yourself on being a good Samaritan.

You can donate your time, money, or both to causes or charities that are making your community a better place. Or take it upon yourself to do some community service, giving your assistance at a local food bank or in numerous other ways to enrich the quality of life for other people in your community. When everyone does their part each and every day to improve their communities, these places become more enjoyable places to live, work, and play.

Multitasking Is A Skill

Sometimes you need to be able to do several things at once. By combining compatible tasks, you can achieve higher productivity. Multitasking is like almost any other art form: it will be continuously improved by practice. How can you improve your ability to multitask? What tasks can be combined? How do you identify compatible tasks?

Let me first introduce you to a concept that I call *thought inertia*. One thought leads to another and another through a connection that leads to the proverbial *train of thought*. It takes a conscious effort to change the train of thought into a sequence of associations and actions. When done effectively, though, it will allow you to complete each task in a sequence of relevance. This will enable you to accomplish all of your tasks in close to the same time it might normally take you to do only one. An example of this would be to go shopping at multiple stores in the same shopping plaza instead of going on different days or different times.

The other is the concept of *muscle memory*. When you learn to do something for the first time, you need to know the procedure. It takes time to do everything because you are framing in your mind the correct steps to take. With a lot of practice, the sequence of steps becomes automatic. Examples of this would be shooting a basketball or swinging a golf club.

Organize Your Day

Organize your day into targeted blocks of ninety minutes to three hours of work, no more, no less. Choose a subject for each block: business development, problem-solving, administration, marketing, production, design, planning, etc. Group your tasks by subject and work on them during the allocated time block. If other ideas arise, keep a small notebook on hand to write them down so you can come back to them at the end of the session or the following day. Then go back to what you were doing. You will find that time will pass by with fewer and fewer thought interruptions. Grouping tasks into themes allows you to focus and have maximum efficiency.

Minimize Context Changes

We call it *multitasking*, but in reality, it's a shortening of time: focus on one task for a while rather than stop to move on to another job. If the functions are very different, it will take time for your brain to move from one task to another. The time required to change context can last anywhere from one to sixty minutes, depending on your concentration, creativity, or analysis and what it takes to complete the task. This is why multitasking is best achieved by grouping similar jobs into themes and running each task in sequential order (one after the other). The time to switch contexts between tasks is minimized, and productivity is maximized.

Take Control of External Interruptions

Responding to external interruptions, such as phone calls, texts, emails, or coworkers, interrupts your concentration and triggers a context change delay. Suppose your context change time is five minutes for each interruption. This amount of time quickly accumulates over the course of a day. Set your voicemail to answer your calls. Close your office door or place a Do Not Disturb sign on the outside. Have discipline to read and respond to email and voicemail a maximum of two or three specific times a day. This should be enough, even for those who expect immediate responses to messages. You may need to reset the expectations of your colleagues or clients by letting them know when you will be available to return their calls. They will appreciate your professionalism.

Dealing with Depression and Anxiety

———— ❧ ————

Life isn't always smooth sailing, even though you do your best to keep it flowing that way. Generally speaking, things out of your control get in the way of your everyday life and create stressful situations you need to address. When these situations start to add on top of one another, you are faced with decisions you'll have to make even though you don't want to. This is where anxiety-caused panic attacks or depressive states come from.

You can understand the difference by realizing where the trigger is coming from. Depression comes from things in your past that you cannot change. Being upset about things in your past is completely normal. We all have things in our past we wish we had done differently or not at all, but it's pointless to allow those past experiences to define your present and future moods. When doing something in the present moment you are afraid to do or that strikes you with fear your adrenaline will start pumping. When you experience this fight-or-flight scenario you need to push through it to accomplish the task. This can include anything from killing a large spider you might be afraid of to climbing a ladder to the second story to clean a window or get on the roof. If your trigger is something you anticipate happening in the future then it's anxiety. We all have future worries: "Will I have enough money to pay rent?" or "Will I get a call back on an application I filled out for a job?" Take a moment to ask yourself why you are having these feelings. When you realize that everything is okay, you'll be able to calm down and think more clearly. Then you can go about fixing the issue before it comes to pass, or at least prepare for it.

Common causes can be from stress in all areas of your life, financial concerns, consumption of alcohol or drugs, and emotional trauma. There are actual symptoms your body and mind experience when you have an anxiety-caused panic attack. These include a sense of impending doom or danger, an increased heart rate, hyperventilation, getting the sweats, abdominal pain, feeling worn out or tired, becoming nervous or restless, and uncontrollable worrying, which leads to trouble concentrating or trying to sleep.

Anxiety is basically the feeling of being trapped with no way out. There is a way out, but in the moment all you can think about are the problems and not the solutions to work out of your anxious state of mind. If you aren't able to beat the anxiety and remain trapped in your current state of mind, then it will lead you into depression. These depressive states can easily compound on one another and become a serious problem if not addressed early on in their development.

Depression is the feeling of continual helplessness in addressing the situations which are currently impacting your life. Most people once seriously depressed require either counseling, medication, or both. I like to say that you need to be your own antidepressant. Realize what triggers your thoughts of helplessness and then try to keep those thoughts in a closed box in the back of your mind. At the same time, realize the things in life you can control and the things that make you the happiest about being alive. If you must, reinforce these positive things in your mind each and every day.

Figure out the things that help you treat your anxiety. Take a moment to try to gain control of your thoughts. For every negative thought you have, try to think of a positive one. Even when times are tough, I'm sure there are numerous things in your life you can be thankful for. Change your environment by going for a walk, drink some cold water, take a cold shower, or call someone you're close with who can help you get your mind off of whatever is causing the panic attack.

These things will be the driving force to help you work your way out of the debilitating forces of an anxiety attack or depressive state. Using this approach, you can beat your anxiety or depressive thoughts anytime you feel them creeping up on you. You now have the power to stay in a controlled frame of mind regardless of how difficult life becomes. There is always a light at the end of the tunnel that is stronger than the darkness you might be experiencing during an anxiety attack or deepened state of depression.

To assist you in your quest to vanquish anxiety and depression from your life, there are several healthy supplements you can take. These include but are not limited to the following:

- Vitamin B complex
- Vitamin D3
- Omega-3s
- Magnesium
- Zinc
- Lavender
- Chamomile

- Spearmint
- Ginger
- Lemon balm
- Valerian root
- 5-HTP — do not overdose, or it could have reverse effects

These supplements are easily found in capsule form, in numerous varieties of teas or essential oils. If cost is an issue, at the very least find a good multivitamin to take. Do your own research on any of these remedies you decide to take. That way you'll learn about their effects and how they will aid in reducing your depression and anxiety symptoms. Choose some of these holistic remedies with a healthy diet, mental fortitude, and control of your emotions through meditation. This should be a great combination of tools to combat your anxiety and depression whenever they occur or as part of a preventative daily routine.

Optimism Vs. Pessimism

———— ༄ଛ୨ ————

In this world, there are two types of people: those who see things in a positive light and those that see them in a negative one. Ask yourself, what kind of person are you? Do you tend to look on the bright side of life, or do you tend to paint situations as dark and troublesome? Are you in control of your life, or is life out to get you? It's easy for other people to see which type of person you are, but can you? Optimists see the glass half full, while pessimists see the glass half empty. Optimists give people the benefit of the doubt, and pessimists are quick to assign blame. Is it really more difficult to see beyond the possibility of evil and into a world of promise and a better life? It all comes down to this: are you pessimistic or optimistic? You can be one or the other, but you cannot be both.

Why can't you be both? People are either one or the other because, in general, your life will be improved or worsened based on how you view circumstances that arise throughout your life. Everything around you is constantly changing, and you will either benefit or falter according to your inner feelings about how to deal with these situations.

The pessimist is the type of person who does not see life with all its beauty and blessings but is filled with many contradictory ideas. They give up easily and lose hope, which is why they feel excluded most of the time. They are hateful and often think they are doing nothing of benefit at all. They blame themselves but also the others around them. They say that the world is a terrible place and that everyone is to blame. These are the people who usually fail in life. They are thrilled to stay where they are and continue to complain about anything that doesn't go their way. Pessimists just enjoy complaining about what's not good in their lives and never do anything to change them.

Optimism Vs. Pessimism

When some people prosper and live happier lives, it is not because they have more than others. They are happy and satisfied with life because they choose to be. They've decided to make their lives as precious as possible. They've realized this is the only way to be happy and hate wasting their time on the things that are not so great in life. They focus on the good things in their life that bring them joy, living life to the fullest, doing their best to make the most of every minute.

Optimists believe in giving people the benefit of the doubt. They recognize the many little things that make them appreciate being alive and seek them daily. They give 100 percent to everything they do, and they love giving their all. They are magically gifted with tons of positive energy and feel excited about experiencing many new and exciting things. They are always on the move and always ready to see what's on the horizon in their life. Optimists are the doers in society.

Pursuit of Improvement

Now think again. Which of these people are you? Of course, we all want to be or become an optimist and have a better outlook on life. You can get a lot of good things if you have a happy heart. This gives you a better opportunity for a healthier and longer life. It gives you a better mood in life and makes you more productive and more efficient. Even if you fail, you don't care as much because you know you did your best, and that's all you expect from every attempt at something new. If you are optimistic, you probably recognize your weaknesses and are already working on trying to become a better person. You will always stand up and strive until you finally succeed. Failures make optimists just work harder to overcome them. Failures are the inspiration to do better, and the optimist knows they will eventually overcome the setbacks and succeed by merely standing up and trying again.

Henry Ford once said, "If you think you can or think you can't, you're right!" Does this mean that what we think, positive or negative, generally happens? The short answer is yes. What the mind can perceive, the mind can achieve. You need to first think you can and then through the belief in yourself and being optimistic of the outcome, start to take the actions necessary to reach your goal. Goals are best achieved by breaking them down into the smallest possible easily accomplished parts. Taking that first step toward your goal is the most important one. Once you accomplish it, you are on the path to accomplishing anything you want. Sometimes goals take years to reach, but without that first step, each sequential step would never happen.

When you add positive and productive action to optimism's driving force, incredible things can happen. You can be as hopeful as you need to be to realize the money for a new car or house, but unless you include productive actions to speed things up, you'll never get there. The difference between *thinking optimistically* and *thinking optimistically while acting productively* is like dreaming verses making that dream a reality.

As we discussed earlier, optimism is the most powerful thing that can guide you on your way to success, even if your problems are almost impossible to overcome. The secret to overcoming such situations lies in your mind and your attitudes. Always remember that nothing is impossible.

As a species we are constantly making the impossible possible with breakthroughs in technology and medicine, to name a few. There are so many things in our world today that even two hundred years ago people would have thought to be impossible. Just because something seems impossible doesn't mean it can't be done if the right person is optimistic enough to take on the challenge.

Optimism or Pessimism: It's Your Choice

There are good reasons to have an optimistic vision. Optimism is associated with a positive outlook and high morale; it will lead you to success in areas such as academia, politics, business, and sports. It is also associated with longevity and reduced stress.

Optimists are no happier than anyone else: they face the same amount of problems and, as such, are no different from others. What is different is how they handle their woes, often the opposite of what one would expect.

The optimist will consider any difficulty as temporary. They see problems as something to learn from. The problematic situation will not deter the optimist, and he will see it as a challenge and take the necessary measures to overcome it. You won't hear an optimist say things like, "I tried it once, and it didn't work. It doesn't make sense to try again."

The positive outlook of optimists also helps them with changes in their lives, such as a sudden tragedy or unexpected event. If they fall, they get back up and continue. There is no stopping a true optimist.

People respond better to those who have a positive attitude. Your outlook on life often spreads to others and can have a significant impact on them. Being optimistic is a desirable quality. Those who display a positive attitude are readily accepted in society, while those who show a pessimistic outlook are often treated less favorably.

In times of stress, optimists generally maintain a state of well-being. Pessimists, on the other hand, often react to stressful events by merely denying their existence or by taking measures to avoid working on the problem, such as procrastinating. For example, they may want to quit smoking, but they always have a reason why they haven't yet.

Studies have indicated that a hopeful viewpoint can help improve the body's natural defensive capabilities, thereby contributing to the ability to fight or recover from illness. Optimists are often healthier than their less optimistic counterparts. They also tend to age slower and may be less prone to common physical diseases in adulthood. They may even live longer than those with less positive outlooks.

Just by becoming more optimistic, you will increase your success rate in everything you do. You'll go through difficult times, like everyone else. But you'll do your best to continue through the hardship and rebound back to normal or even better than you were before. That is the true nature of what it means to be an optimist.

The Right Way to Judge Others

Most people are inherently good and live their lives without hate or a dislike for others around them. They are overwhelmingly caring, helpful, and peaceful. See those around you as equal human beings regardless of the color of their skin, on the same journey through life as you are. Don't use color to describe people; use their official classification. If you must talk about race, use the terms African American, Hispanic, Asian, Indian, African, Pacific Islander, Native American, or Caucasian.

You should never judge anyone based on their race, gender, beliefs, or political views. This can sometimes be difficult based on previous experiences you've had with a certain group of people, but you can't ultimately be prepared for your future interactions with people of a similar likeness, so each and every time you meet someone new, they should be assessed

The Right Way to Judge Others

singularly and with a clean slate. People should only be judged on their merits and not attributes they can't change.

To a small degree, we all involuntarily judge people around us whether we know we are doing it or not. It's an automatic response, and usually we start this process from the moment we see them. Are they young or old, tall or short, overweight or skinny, and at the same time we're rating their level of attractiveness and if they might do us harm. This quick, overall physical way of seeing people is only a very small part of how you should view the people around you. More importantly are the things about people you can't know about them simply from a quick glance.

People's words and actions are much more important factors in your overall judgment of them. Do they project confidence with their tone when they speak? Or is their tone more quiet and reserved? Are they passive or aggressive? Do their actions benefit you or hinder you? These are just a few questions to ask yourself when assessing someone new who has entered your life either from school, work, an activity, or in passing.

Judgments should be held until after you get to know each person individually, after you have spoken to them and seen how they act toward you and the others around you. Actions are the most important thing you should judge people on. Words can be misunderstood or taken out of context, when said sarcastically or comically, but an action is a planned motion by a person to reach a result. If a person's action doesn't align with a similar action you would take yourself, then and only then should you judge that person on what they did.

If someone does something that doesn't align with your values and you feel like you want to correct that action, calmly go over and speak to that person about what they are doing and find out why they are acting that way. Then after you know what their thought process is, you can let them know how you feel about it and what they can do differently in the future not to offend you or anyone else. If no middle ground can be found, in some cases the best solution is simply to agree to disagree.

You'll be very surprised how many amazing people are around you when you view them as equals and leave judgment out of the equation, unless actual actions are taken to disrupt your initial optimistic view of them. You should essentially give all people the benefit of the doubt of being a good person when judging their overall character, unless proven otherwise. It's not that there are no bad apples out there, but they are few and far between. Most of society is just trying to get through their day peacefully.

Understanding & Accepting Religion in Society

Religion has taken many forms over the centuries. Different cultures have chosen how to represent the unexplainable forces around us. Some cultures have many gods, each with their own dominion over certain aspects of life, and others have an almighty God who rules over all. The great thing about whatever you believe is that your understanding of why things happen is unique to you. Religion is an interpretation of your inner feelings and how you fit into the universe as a whole. Some people choose to be more religious, others choose to be less religious, and a select few choose to believe in nothing at all.

We can all choose to pray or not pray in our own way. None of these choices is right or wrong. They are simply personal choices of how to explain the age-old question of what happened to create life in the cosmos, eventually allowing humans to inherit the planet earth and giving them the innate ability to be intelligent beings. Depending on what God or gods you believe in, you can feel they have complete control over your path through life and death, or that they don't influence your daily life at all.

I like to think something in the middle of both. God is all-powerful, sees all, and is in all places at once. It's possible prayer is stronger when done in a place of worship with others, but it can just as easily be done anywhere you are. Prayer may or may not have any effect at all, depending on how you pray for the changes to your current situation. My everyday choices are my own free will, but the most important experiences I'm destined to have, good and bad, were preplanned at birth. Then when I'm no longer needed to do whatever it is I was meant to do, I'll pass onto the next life.

One of my favorite allusions to religion which everyone who's seen it can relate to, is the Force from *Star Wars*. It's an energy field created by all living things. It surrounds us, penetrates us, and binds the galaxy together. You can believe it's real or not, but either way you're a part of its all-encompassing nature.

For those who don't believe in religion, I hate to break it to you, but you are believing in something. You are believing in your creation as an accidental occurrence through the evolution of things from nothing at all. What are the odds of that? It is totally up to you to feel that way, but please let others think about what they feel is best for them to believe in as well.

Handling Addictions and Bad Habits

We all have our addictions. Some are healthy and benefit our lives, but most are damaging to our mental abilities and physical health. These harmful addictions seriously hinder our ability to be more productive members of society.

When using drugs like cocaine or methamphetamine, your senses will become numb, and your brain will get fried over time. These substances will cause you anxiety and insomnia, among other serious side effects. When using marijuana, it will dumb you down and sap your energy and ability to get important work done. Drinking too much alcohol impairs your ability to make good decisions and even walk straight. The hangover you'll have in the morning will keep you from being productive the following day. Using any of these substances and countless others, including abusing prescription medicines, will cause you to lose control of your normal mental acuteness, and some affect your physical capabilities as well.

Dopamine is a neurotransmitter and a chemical responsible for signaling nerve cells in the brain. It becomes activated whenever something good happens to you, such as knowing it's time to eat, finishing a project, or the instant gratification of such simple things as getting a text message or app notification, etc. This means you can also get dopamine from physical exercise, playing video games, having sex or masturbating, using drugs and any other rewarding occurrence in your life. Understanding dopamine response and knowing how your mind works is the first step to breaking a bad addiction.

The second step is elimination. You must eliminate the addictive thing from your life. Don't buy the alcohol, drugs, prescription pills, or cigarettes, so they are not within arm's reach when you get a craving. If you're trying to get work done, put your phone on silent or airplane mode, have someone you trust hide your video game controller, and set up a parental block on your personal computer so you can't visit explicit sites.

The third step is replacement. Whenever you get the urge to do the bad habit, you need to have something to replace the action with. If you are trying to cut back on the time you spend playing video games, then when your allotted time is up, grab a book to read or go do an outdoor activity. If you are trying to break a bad habit of smoking, put gum in your mouth every time you get the "I need a cigarette" sensation. There is even gum with nicotine in it, so you can break the habit of actually smoking a cigarette before you break your dependence on the feeling of nicotine. Then after you form the better habit of putting gum in your mouth every day, you can more easily switch to gum that doesn't have the nicotine in it and replace the nicotine with another stimulant like caffeine. Even better would be to work with a nutritionist to improve your energy naturally. If you've been addicted to something for a long time that's been harming your health since you started, you'd be surprised how a healthy body feels when it's not being bombarded continuously with harmful substances. Obviously, the worse the habit has become or the longer you've been doing it, the more difficult this step will be for you.

The last step is triumph. This only occurs when you have conquered the addiction and it's no longer part of your life. When you think about the control it had over you in the past, there is no care in your mind to ever experience it again, and in fact, just thinking about it revolts you.

Regardless of the addiction you are trying to break, using these steps will help you triumph over it.

Having Successful Relationships

---- ∞ ----

As we go through life, we are constantly forming relationships. We meet people at school, through activities, through being out in the community, and at work. We pass by most people without a thought of engagement. That engagement is a necessity when building a relationship. The more we engage with others, the easier it is for us to form relationships.

Not all relationships are created equal. We have our acquaintances, friends, true friends, and family. Acquaintances are people we interact with every day but have no real connection to. Friends are people we enjoy being around and plan to spend our time with. True friends are people we welcome into our lives and treat almost as if they are family. Here's the thing about true friends: you don't pick them, they pick you. Family are the people you've grown up around who care about you no matter what.

Pursuit of Improvement

When trying to find that special someone for an intimate and long-lasting relationship, you must understand that everyone has faults. No one is perfect, and no relationship will ever be perfect. It's great to dream about finding someone who checks off all your boxes and truly completes you, but the idea of a fairy-tale relationship is just that: a fairy tale. You may experience fleeting moments of fairy- tale-like perfection with that person, but those moments will be few and far between. The best way to go about finding a long-term partner is to find someone you really enjoy being around and someone who you feel cares about you as much as you care about them.

Be very protective of who you give your heart to. All too often I see people in unhealthy intimate long-term relationships. It's difficult to end things when you feel you love someone, but if they are doing anything to harm you physically, mentally, or emotionally, it's time to get out of that situation and be on your own for a bit. When the heartbreak subsides over the next couple of weeks, you'll realize you're better off without them in your life, and you can start engaging with other people again who will treat you better.

Learning to Think for Yourself

The world is full of businesses and people trying their hardest to influence your feeling and actions. There are always two differing points of view and a little gray area in between. It's your job to figure out which side you want to be on. When there is no great choice, break down the pluses and minuses of both and then vote your values. Don't take everything you hear as the whole truth on the matter. Take a look at both sides and decide for yourself how you feel about the person, product, or situation.

On the business side, companies are spending millions of dollars to win you over so you will become brand loyal to them. Think about the people who only wear Under Armour clothes and shoes. Sometime in the past, there was an advertisement that influenced them enough to buy an Under Armour product, and because they enjoyed using the product, they continued to buy more from the same brand. This holds true for everything from fast food to cars, computers, restaurants, etc. The biggest companies in the world may not be the best for you, but they have influenced millions of other people to think they are the best for them.

Whether it's family, friends, acquaintances, or people you see on social media and TV, the people in your life are constantly trying to influence you. Anyone and everyone in your life, especially the people on news programs, are trying to make you think a certain way. It's necessary to first understand what is being said and then to take a moment to decide if you really agree with what's being told to you. It's best to look at both arguments objectively and then determine which you feel is right based on your own feelings and experiences.

When you start to understand the reasons for the points of view taken by businesses and individuals, it will open your mind to make better decisions for yourself in the future. Motive is the basis for so much of how things are phrased. For example, say a good deed was done, and instead of just complementing the good deed and being happy with the result, someone says that the good deed wasn't enough and more could have been done. What is their motive for saying such a thing?

Whenever you receive information, it should go through a filtering process as to where the information came from, who said it, and what motive they may have for saying what they said. Don't allow yourself to be sold by manipulating ads or twisted truths. If after you've done your due diligence you understand the truth behind the information, you can choose to believe it as credible or not.

Transition from Your Past Self into An Improved Version of Yourself

―――― ∽≈∽ ――――

We all have the ability to commit ourselves to continuous personal improvement. Trust me, it's worth every moment you spend to become a better version of yourself. Also, it can help you become more advanced and productive in other areas of your life too. It's something you can do to any degree, anytime in your life.

We all have room for improvement. Here are the beginning steps to becoming a superior version of yourself:

Decide to change. Many people think they are perfect as they are and do not feel the need to change, improve or develop. But in life, if you stay still, you stay behind. If you don't improve or grow, you won't progress. Open-minded people are always ready to change, and they are willing to invest time and effort in themselves.

Become more aware of your faults. In the event you want to improve as a person, self-awareness is a great place to start. Evaluate your behavior, evaluate your actions, and weigh the reactions you receive. Attempt to see yourself through the eyes of those around you and ask yourself where you need to improve.

Set an example of yourself as a model for the other people in your life. This awareness will encourage you to do your best and maintain the highest level of integrity so as not to disappoint those who admire you.

Control your temper. Any statement of outrage is an indication of a lack of emotional control. Passion is a universal human trait, but it is a relentless, useless, and self-destructive quality. If you give in to anger, you hurt yourself more than anyone else. If your issue is stressful, practice anger management techniques like taking a deep breath and counting backward from ten when you feel like you might burst out with emotion. Saying or doing something you will regret seconds later is easy to prevent when you learn to control your emotions.

Practice radical honesty. I am a big supporter of coming clean, the whole truth, and nothing but the truth. Honesty in compassion is one of the main characteristics of a person improving themselves, because any communication full of lies will make people lose respect for you.

Find ways to be helpful. Helping others is one of the best ways to become a better person. When you support someone who needs it, you realize it can be useful for other people and that you have a role to play in adding more to the world.

Show people you love them. Showing people you love and care for them builds relationships and trust that drive them to love better as well. It also makes them happy, which is likely to spread to others too.

Which Version of Yourself Are You Living?

Throughout life, we are continually inventing and reinventing ourselves. And if you look back, there are probably some versions of you that you like more than others. Hopefully, the most recent version of yourself is the most mature and refined up until now, but that is not always the case.

Most of the time, when we set out to change something important to us, it is because we're distraught in a specific area. It could be with well-being, ability to connect with others, budgeting correctly, certain activities we enjoy, or something completely different. Suggesting to ourselves that the old variant needs improvement, we are trusting that through working on these areas, we will have the chance to show incremental improvements over time. For instance, suppose that one day you stand on the scale and the number that gazes back at you is a lot higher than you want it to be. Right then and there, you decide to make serious changes in your life to help you lose the weight. That is just one example of seeing a necessary improvement and acting on it.

At that moment, you are inspired to drive the number on the scale down to a more acceptable one. You will now act differently going forward and have a solid inspiration each day to eat better and control your unhealthy cravings. You start heading off to the rec center. You begin eating servings of mixed greens and drinking shakes like they are your new daily treat. What's more, after some time, you begin to see that number on the scale go down, and your favorite pair of jeans are starting to fit again. After some time, you notice how much better you feel, the amount of vitality you have, and how it was all worthwhile. Before you know it, another form of you has developed and improved.

Once you reveal this new best you to yourself, you'll generally be propelled to eat better, exercise, and carry on with a progressively dynamic way of life. You know the drill from now on. The past adaptation of yourself, the one that made the decision to eat better and be gradually active, has diminished into nothing, is smothered completely. You accept that the old adaptation of you is gone until the end of time. Be that as it may, the person in question is still there—and will consistently be there, remaining, hanging tight for the perfect minute to hop into the game once again, regardless of whether you want it to or not. As you progress through life, you will have visions of past adaptations of yourself, and you need to be vigilant not to allow your bad habits of the past to resurface. The former you that wasn't so pleasant to other people. The past you that did things you weren't proud of. The past you who never watched what they ate. The former you that ate appallingly and never worked out. The history of you that was enormously effective in changing who that past person was and how they have been transformed into the current and best version of you that you are today.

These past forms of yourself are still with you. Their DNA has been inked onto your mind, and there is no real way to free them from your life. As you progress through life, you may have many various forms of yourself going around in your mind. Regardless, all that truly matters is the ability to essentially keep working on yourself and improving in areas you feel you are lacking.

Fortunately, the more you love the new you, the harder it will be to find your old self and the quieter the inner dialogue will be. Your new habits will become your new normal, and you will have successfully completed your transformation.

The only way to progress consistently in creating and maintaining a new version of yourself is awareness.

Monitoring yourself is the initial step to moving from the old to the new. But more importantly, it is this awareness of the person that will keep you on track and prevent you from returning to your old habits and your previous state of being.

Over time, with persistent effort, older versions of you will begin to lose their voice, and a new, stronger, more consistent version of you will become the dominant voice in your head that speaks louder and more precisely and guides you in the direction you want to go.

www.ingramcontent.com/pod-product-compliance
Lightning Source LLC
Chambersburg PA
CBHW061310110426
42742CB00012BA/2131